BEYOND A REASONABLE DOUBT

A Case for Common Sense Christianity

LARRY SIEKAWITCH

Is there evidence for God and Jesus? You might be surprised...

PAGE PUBLISHING, INC.
Conneaut Lake, PA

First originally published by Page Publishing 2020

ISBN 978-1-6624-2438-0 (pbk)
ISBN 978-1-6624-2439-7 (digital)

Printed in the United States of America

CONTENTS

INTRODUCTION

Hello, normal human being. I invite you to a discussion concerning God and ultimate things that really matter. I am a big fan of Peanut Buster Parfaits, but if the world did not have such delectable treats, it would still survive. On the other hand, it is kind of important whether God exists or not. This won't take long, and it won't be overly complicated. Philosophers make a living on overcomplicating things; I will try not to. I want to appeal to common sense and to the basic jurisprudence of our land, innocent until proven guilty, and the evidence must be beyond a reasonable doubt. First, we must discuss whether there are basic truths that are self-evident. Second, we will need to examine what some of these self-evident truths are. Third, for the bulk of this work, we will briefly look at some evidence for God's existence and the truth of Christianity. Next, we will see how common sense can help us understand the Bible better. Finally, we will examine one argument against God that appears to be the atomic bomb of the atheist—the problem of evil and suffering. First, let's look at common sense.

COMMON SENSE

I heard of a man who thought he was dead. His psychologist attempted to help him to no avail, until he came up with an idea. He thought that if he could convince the man that dead men don't bleed, he could have success. So he went through a battery of tests and biology books proving to the man that dead men don't bleed. Until finally, the man said, "Of course, dead men don't bleed." At that moment, the psychologist then poked him with a sharp instrument, causing him to bleed, to which he replied, "Wow! I guess dead men do bleed." There are those on the fringe of society that refuse to believe anything that goes against what they already believe no matter how much evidence you show them. They are even willing to go against common sense. Rene Descartes is famous for saying, "I think therefore I am."[1] This phrase reminds me of another joke, but we will have to press on. Descartes felt like it was necessary to prove anything before you could believe it. But is this really necessary? I don't test every chair before I sit in it to see whether it has the capacity to hold me up or not. I trust that it will hold me up, unless it really looks bad. It is possible that I could be wrong every now and then, but it is simply not worth checking every detail all the time before sitting. Whether Descartes emphasized reason too much or got the cart before the horse is not what really matters. What he reveals without knowing it is that there are certain truths that seem real and simply do not need rational defense *ad nauseam*. One could say to him that just because I think doesn't really prove that you think, because you could just be a figment of my imagination (pretty good imagination, huh?). I could have been born one day ago with all the memories

---

[1] *Cogito ergo sum*

7

implanted in me. This could really be *The Matrix*! But we simply can't live like that. At least normal people can't and shouldn't.

In philosophical terms, what I am talking about is akin to Scottish commonsense realism, which argued against the overly skeptical philosophies of the likes of David Hume, etc. Have you ever met someone who was brilliant when it came to philosophy, science, or some other field of study but just simply had no common sense at all? The founding fathers of the US believed in this commonsense realism. The Declaration of Independence specifically states the following: "We hold these truths to be self-evident, that all men are created equal, that they are endowed by their Creator with certain unalienable Rights, that among these are Life, Liberty and the pursuit of Happiness." When it says the truths are self-evident, it is appealing to common sense that does not need to be rationally proved before normal people embrace it. Wacko skeptics are excluded, but the average person on the street shows his or her intelligence when he or she accepts this great statement our country was founded on. I think common sense can be applied to religion, but it might not come out like you first expect. Let's give it a try.

Self-Evident Truths

Are there basic, self-evident truths? I love the dilemma of empiricism. It states that only facts derived from empirical evidence can be seen as true; that which we can observe through the five senses is the only thing allowable for verification or falsification of truth. The problem with empiricism is that the argument itself is stated outside any empirical evidence. It is not empirically evident that empiricism is true, but it does seem reasonable that empirical evidence goes a long way in establishing some forms of truth. The law of gravity is a great example (gravity is the law; it's not just a good idea). It is true that through observation, gravity works. The earth literally sucks! But how do we know that this will still be true tomorrow? We can't prove that gravity will work in the future, but we would be foolish to reject it simply because it can't be proven. The continuation of the laws of nature is actually an example of a self-evident truth.

What are some self-evident truths? Let's start out with the Declaration of Independence. It says that all people are created equal. Is this true? People do not all have the same privileges. Many people get lousy breaks, whereas a few seem to be as lucky as a leprechaun (leprechauns are not self-evident). But deep down, when we take away our selfishness, most will admit that it does seem to be true that everybody as people are equal and should be shown dignity and respect. The Bible wholeheartedly agrees with this idea when it says that all people are created in the image of God (Genesis 1:27). The Bible is full of these commonsense ideas. Interestingly, other religions seem to be deficient in this area (my opinion from research). If all people are created in the image of God, then it makes sense that everyone deserves the same respect and dignity as everyone else, no matter what their social status, economic situation, color, race, etc. This, by the way is why Christianity is, by far, the most ethnically diverse religion on the planet and also why it was Christians who stepped in to stop slavery in England and America. It is also why it is Christians who demand the same equal rights to little babies who haven't been born yet. All people are created equal.

Who is going to argue with the self-evident truth that all people are created equal? It cannot be proven with philosophy or reason. It goes against Darwinian evolution, which calls for survival of the fittest. It is no surprise that Hitler appealed to evolution in his attempt to form the super race. Darwin himself was a racist. Why shouldn't superior races select out the inferior ones? Because we all know deep down inside that all people are created equal.

The Declaration of Independence also states that we were endowed by our Creator with the inalienable rights of life, liberty, and the pursuit of happiness (in that order). Notice it is suggesting that another self-evident truth is that we have a Creator. Not all of our founding fathers were Christians, but they all believed in some form of supreme being who created us. Is this self-evident? I'm going to attempt to make a case for yes to this question later, but once again, it does agree with the Bible. The first verse in the Bible, Genesis 1:1, assumes the existence of God without attempting to prove it when it says "In the beginning God created the heavens and the earth." Romans 1:19–20 says, "Since what can be known about God is *evident* among them, because God has shown it to them. For His invisible attributes, that is, His eternal power and divine nature, have been clearly seen since the creation of the world, being understood through what He has made (emphasis mine)."

Another self-evident truth, not found in the Declaration of Independence, is the reality of love. No one can prove love exists. We even have a hard time defining love, but we all know deep down that love exists, and it is more than neurons firing in the brain due to genetic engineering. Atheist philosophers can argue in their ivory towers about the nonexistence of love or freedom or God's existence, but normal people dismiss their ramblings as having a lack of common sense.

Another self-evident truth is freedom of the will. Determinist psychologists like B. F. Skinner demand that we are not actually free (I think they were determined to say that). They say that we are determined by our genetic makeup and past circumstances and don't really have the ability to make a free decision. We are all robots that think we have freedom. But most of us know that when we come to a decision in life, even the really tough decisions like whether to get Little Caesars pizza or Papa John's, we actually have freedom to choose. We have free will. Sure, our will has pressures on it from our background and genetic makeup, but our individual circumstances and biological disposition do not make up all of who we are. We are more than the sum of our parts. As humans, we are unique to the animal kingdom on this planet (we won't talk about the potential of life on other planets because it is not self-evident). Once again, freedom of the will fits very well with the biblical model that states we were created in God's image and therefore unique in all of creation.

I believe that the idea that we live beyond the grave is self-evident. Humans have prepared for an afterlife throughout our existence according to anthropologists, who define a religious propensity as one of the unique qualities of Homo sapiens. C. S. Lewis put it this way: "If I find in myself desires which nothing in this world can satisfy, the only logical explanation is that I was made for another world."[2] Ecclesiastes 3:11 declares, "He has made everything appropriate in its time. He has also put eternity in their hearts, but man cannot discover the work God has done from beginning to end."

Are these things self-evident? If equality, love, free will, God's existence, and life after death are self-evident, then we must also surmise that humans are more than physical beings. According to atheist materialists, most of the universe's history existed without consciousness or intelligence, yet here it is in humans. *Poof!* Abracadabra. Douglas Groothuis quotes materialist Colin McGinn: "The bond between mind and the brain is a deep mystery. Moreover, it is an ultimate mystery, a mystery that human intelligence will never unravel."[3] The mind is different from the brain yet works in conjunction with it. Groothuis notes below:

> Mental states and physical states differ in kind, not in degree. Thus they cannot be identical, given this very simple principle of identity: whatever differs *in kind* cannot be identical. There is no metaphysical halfway house between mental and physical states. There is no graduated spectrum of states *between* the mental and the physical. In fact, mental states lack the *defining properties* of physical states, and physical states lack the *defining properties* of mental states. Contradictory properties cannot attach to the same thing. As Leibniz noted, if we liken the human brain to a factory, we could see any number of movable parts, but we could never see the thinking itself [emphasis original].[4]

Thoughts are not measurable because they are not physical. Thoughts are immaterial. But how do we explain where conscious-

[2] C. S. Lewis, *Mere Christianity* (New York: Harper Collins, 1980), 136–137.
[3] Douglas Groothuis, *Christian Apologetics* (Downers Grove, IVP, 2011), 391.
[4] Ibid., 395.

ness and intelligence come from? Common sense tells us that there is an immaterial aspect of who we are. We have a soul and a body, both an immaterial and material aspect to who we are as humans (dualism). But where did the soul come from? Common sense would tell us the soul came from an immaterial source—God!

Now just because commonsense people believe these things, that doesn't mean they are true. But if there is corroborating evidence, we should give these ideas the benefit of the doubt. If that is true, we should be allowed to talk about them in public settings, even in school, government events, and politics, because most commonsense people believe these ideas to be true. Atheists should not be allowed to dominate the discussion by silencing the conversation before it takes place. If the evidence points away from the existence of God, then we should abandon the hypothesis, but if it agrees with the commonsense ideas that we have discussed, then let's give God the benefit of the doubt.

Beyond a Reasonable Doubt

In the United States, one is innocent until proven guilty. This concept was developed to ensure only guilty people were punished. It started from Roman Justinian codes and English common law and was embraced by America and the United Nations later on. It seems like a fair way to go about legal stuff. Tragically, it was not enforced in many cases of our history, especially toward minorities, which reveals that though "all humans are created equal" is self-evident, many humans don't live out this concept because we are bad. The fact that we need a judicial system in the first place backs up the biblical concept of the sinful and corrupt nature of humanity. Just how bad we are is up for debate, but the fact that we are all bad seems self-evident.

We are innocent until proven guilty, and guilt must be established beyond a reasonable doubt. We have lawyers, juries, defendants, etc. to see if there is enough evidence to throw the guy in the slammer or not. Beyond a reasonable doubt is different from beyond a shadow of a doubt. When all the evidence is seen, if it seems reasonable that the person is guilty and unreasonable that he or she is innocent, then the verdict of guilty is made. It is possible that a Martian came down and stopped time to do the crime and then started time with the gun in the hands of an innocent bystander, but it is not probable. Fingerprints, DNA, and eyewitnesses go a long way as far as evidence goes. But the burden of proof is on the prosecutor, not the defendant, because we are innocent until proven guilty. Now, what does this have to do with our subject? Some argue that God's existence must be proven beyond the shadow of a doubt. Others argue as if the concept that God exists is wrong until proven right. I believe both of these statements are false. Since humanity has always believed in a supreme being, it seems reasonable that God's existence should be given the benefit of the doubt, innocent until proven guilty, true until proven false. But most atheists don't think this way, so I am willing to show that God's existence is true beyond a reasonable doubt. There is enough evidence to reveal that God exists to the normal human who doesn't want to get duped but also is open to the idea if enough evidence is available, but there is not enough evidence to force the unwilling to capitulate. I think God was brilliant in revealing just enough for the honest seeker, but not enough for the hardened flat-earther set in his or her ways. What I want to do now is to present a case for God's existence and then a case for Christianity to see if it coincides with common sense. We need to examine the evidence in detail. What if I am pulling the wool over your eyes? Is there detailed evidence for these claims? You betcha! I am from Minnesota, and the accent comes out when I get excited. The rest of this book will examine the evidence.

A CASE FOR GOD

From an intellectual standpoint, is it possible for an intelligent atheist to become a Christian? I will attempt to briefly describe the steps taken in three parts: First, how an atheist can move toward agnosticism, then how an agnostic can embrace theism, and finally how a theist can become a Christian without having to check his or her brain in at the door.

Atheism is self-defeating. For an atheist to claim that he or she knows for sure that there is no God, he or she would have to have all knowledge; otherwise, it is possible outside his or her limited knowledge that there is evidence for the existence of a God (see diagram A). If the atheist had all knowledge, he or she would be God because omniscience is an attribute of God alone. Imagine God denying God's existence. If the person is human, he or she doesn't know everything and so must conclude that it is possible, perhaps only remotely possible, but possible nonetheless that there is

a God. This is why every intelligent atheist should convert to agnosticism, which is the belief that one does not know if there is a God or not, even if he or she leans toward the negative possibility. Most atheists today recognize this problem and redefine the word *atheist* to mean something similar to what in the past has been defined as agnosticism. They are getting smarter, but there is no reason to reinvent the wheel. Just admit you are wrong and you are agnostic. Atheists have a really hard time admitting they are wrong.

Agnosticism is a more intelligent belief system than atheism, but agnosticism doesn't go far enough. If you are not sure whether there is a God or not, three powerful arguments should be considered. I do not claim that these are absolute arguments; a skeptic can always find a way around them. But the real question is, "What is the most likely truth after considering these arguments?" Use common sense! One telltale flaw in many agnostics and atheists is that they do not read opposing material with an open mind (kind of like Republicans and Democrats). There is quite often an ulterior motive for their skepticism. When I press the person for further information, many times, I discover that the person has experienced some deep pain, which skewed his or her belief in a benevolent god. I find that the person is actually mad at God rather than in disbelief of His existence. This is certainly not the case for all people, but it is a warning that we might want to question why we believe something. Is it based on the facts drawn from an objective investigation, or is it a belief we hold because we are running away from something? Let's briefly look at the three powerful arguments to see if they have potential for holding water (for you literalists, holding water is a metaphor for the soundness of the argument).

The Cosmological Argument

First, the cosmological argument states that something must be eternal, either the universe or the creator of the universe. There are exactly three possible options concerning the universe (see Universe Options Chart): it caused itself, it is eternal and therefore was never caused, or something outside the universe that is eternal caused the universe. Some clever atheists are actually espousing the first option. They declare that the universe inevitably caused itself—creation out of nothing from nothing. Commonsense people reject this option because in order for the universe to poof itself into existence, it would already have to exist to

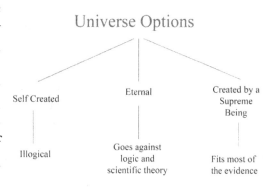

do the poofing (poofing is a technical term for creating). I find it simply amazing that some are going to this extent to outsource God. You have to wonder if there is an ulterior motive for these supposed scientists to postulate such a silly idea. Perhaps they don't want a boss.

The second option is that the universe is eternal and therefore doesn't need a creator. There is a philosophical problem with this option as well as a scientific one. Philosophically, it doesn't make sense that there is an eternal progression in the past of finite cause-and-effect phenomena. We would never be able to get to where we are today if there was no beginning. Scientifically, the latest accepted science recognizes that the universe had a beginning. It appears that both philosophically and scientifically, it makes good sense to believe the universe is not eternal. We will examine this second option in more detail in just a moment.

The third option is that there is an eternal nonphysical Creator who started everything. If the universe is not eternal, then it must have a creator; that creator is the all-powerful God. Something has to be eternal as we saw in rejecting the first option. The universe isn't eternal as we saw in the second option. Therefore, it seems most likely that our common sense, self-evident hypothesis of a supreme being is correct.

In this first argument, you may have noticed, if you are a philosophy buff, that I have used an inductive approach rather than a deductive approach to the problem. Let me explain for all non-philosophy majors. Deductive arguments are usually placed in the form of a syllogism and, if correct, are full-proof arguments. Here is an example used in most philosophy textbooks:

1. All men are mortal.
2. Socrates is a man.
3. Therefore, Socrates is mortal.

Notice that if the first two premises are correct, the conclusion must be true. I could have stated my argument above in a deductive form. What philosophers call the Kalam cosmological argument is usually presented deductively as follows:

1. Whatever begins to exist has a cause (law of cause and effect).
2. The universe began to exist (based on philosophical and scientific evidence).
3. Therefore, the universe has a cause (contra eternal universe).
4. That uncaused cause of the universe is God (something must be eternal and therefore uncaused).[5]

The plus side of deductive arguments is that they are very persuasive if correct. But the downside of the deductive argument is that if you can come up with any possibility, no matter how remote that might be an alternative explanation, the whole argument is destroyed. An inductive argument states the rational case for an argument in such a way that what really matters is what is most likely true after all the facts are presented. Is it beyond a reasonable doubt?

I have an atheist friend named Tom. He is stuck in deductive mode like many of the professional evangelistic atheists of our day. You might be asking, "There are evangelistic atheists?" It is actually quite a profession. Men like Richard Dawkins, Dan Barker, and

---

[5] Two great presentations for this argument can be found in Douglas Groothius, *Christian Apologetics* (Downers Grove: IVP, 2011), chapter 11 and William Lane Craig, *Reasonable Faith* (Wheaton: Crossway Books, 2008), chapter 3.

Christopher Hitchens (Hitchens died, so he is no longer an atheist) make a lot of money off this trade. You might ask, "Why would an atheist be evangelistic?" They say they hate Christians. I have met some Christians that would cause some to dislike us, but most are good people and certainly don't push people to become evangelistic atheists. The only thing I can think of is that there is a devil who has them in his control (1 John 5:19 and my opinion). Anyway, back to Tom. Tom says that the universe could have been made by an infinite universe popping machine or the spaghetti monster. He admits there is no evidence for either postulation. I use the inductive method in order to show that though there might be some slight possibility of an alternative theory. The evidence leans heavily in the direction of a supreme being. We haven't proved the Christian God yet, but let's see if the two premises "whatever begins to exist has a cause" and "the universe began to exist" are reasonable.

Whatever begins to exist has a cause. This premise relies on the scientific principle of cause and effect, which states, "Every cause has a prior effect." Science would be impossible without this principle. An amazing philosophical book called *Because A Little Bug Went Ka-choo!*[6] illustrates the law of cause and effect. This remarkable book illustrates (with great pictures) how each effect has a cause behind it. A little bug sneezed and eventually caused a giant parade. We either have an eternal number of contingent (I'll explain this word later) cause-and-effect episodes going back forever in the past, or there was a first uncaused cause. Thomas Aquinas gave us several variations of this argument, and the medieval Muslims gave us the Kalam argument mentioned above.

I need to explain a couple things at this point. First, the premise says, "Whatever *begins* to exist has a cause." It doesn't say everything has a cause. It should be pretty obvious that the first cause doesn't have a cause; otherwise, it wouldn't be the first one. Kids sometimes ask the profound philosophical question, "Who made God?" This is a wonderful opportunity for parents to explain to the child (or grown-up) that God is eternal and so was never made. Something

---

[6] *Because A Little Bug Went Ka-choo!* (New York: Random House, 1975).

has to be eternal. It is either the universe or the cause of the universe, but something has to be eternal, our uncaused cause (unpoofed poofer for the more sophisticated). Second, we need to understand the concept of contingency. To be contingent means something is possible but not necessary, and it is dependent on something else. Every effect is contingent on the previous cause; it is not necessary. It is possible that it didn't occur if other circumstances were true, and it is dependent on the cause. Ronald Nash makes a great observation: "If every part of the world (past, present, and future) is contingent, it certainly makes sense to regard the entire world as contingent." But if the whole universe is contingent, then it must be dependent on something outside itself—a noncontingent, eternal Being. But how do we know if the universe had a beginning? Let's look at the second premise.

Premise two states, "The universe began to exist." Believe it or not, most scientists before Einstein and Hubble used to think the universe was eternal. It was in what they called a steady state. But as I have suggested, this seems both illogical and contrary to the latest scientific theory. How is it illogical? Think about it, can you count to infinity? Go ahead and start to see if you can. I'm waiting. You would never stop and actually reach infinity, would you? This is because an actual infinite is impossible. Now if the universe has been around for infinity (no beginning), it would have already reached infinity, an actual infinite, because it has been going on for infinity in the past. Do you see the problem? There is infinite set theory in mathematics, but no actual infinites in the universe. Imagine you have an infinite number of golf balls (this would be very helpful for me since I lose several each outing). Half are white, and half are yellow. You give all the yellow golf balls to your friend because you hate those things, especially in the fall because they get lost in the leaves. How many golf balls do you have? You would have the same amount, infinity. How can you give half of them away and not lose any? It doesn't make sense because actual infinites are an illogical impossibility. But if the universe is infinite in time with an infinite number of contingent cause-and-effect episodes, you would have an actual infinite, which logically appears to be impossible. Something both outside the universe's space and its time must have caused it to exist.

Some have claimed God as an actual infinite with the same problem as the world, but God is simple and outside time. According to Einstein's theory of relativity, time and matter are interconnected and began at the same time. Time itself was created! It is impossible for us finite creatures to imagine timelessness, but that doesn't mean timelessness is impossible. If God is timeless outside our space and time and created both space and time, then it all makes sense. Here is an illustration that helps me (but if it doesn't help you, then just forget it and take two aspirins): We are three-dimensional beings, four dimensions if we include time as a dimension. Imagine if we came across two-dimensional beings, the Flat People. We could walk right up to them, and they could not see us. We could even harass them by putting our hand into their dimension and hit them without them even seeing where it came from. What if God is multidimensional? He could interact with us in our three dimensions and time without being bound to those dimensions. Once again, if you have a headache, take two aspirins.

It seems illogical for the universe to be eternal. It also goes against the latest scientific theory. Many Christians are opposed to the Big Bang theory, but if it is true, it actually proves the universe had a beginning; God said "Bang!" and there it was. The Big Bang theory doesn't prove evolution (we will get to that later). Hugh Ross presents us with the Big Bang fundamentals:

> Many big bang theories exist. What they all share, however, are three fundamental characteristics: (1) a transcendent cosmic beginning that occurred a finite time ago; (2) a continuous, universal cosmic expansion; and (3) a cosmic cooling from an extremely hot initial state.[7]

[7] Hugh Ross, *The Creator and the Cosmos* 4th edition (RTB Press, Covina CA, 2018), 28.

What's fascinating about this discovery is that it actually agrees with the Bible without any contradiction. Genesis 1:1 declares the universe had a finite beginning in the past. Isaiah 40:22 agrees with the universal cosmic expansion: "God is enthroned above the circle of the earth; its inhabitants are like grasshoppers. He stretches out the heavens like thin cloth and spreads them out like a tent to live in." The Big Bang theory is based on three observations: (1) The second law of thermodynamics. This law states that the universe is moving toward a state of entropy where the amount of usable energy will eventually run out. The stars are burning out and will be gone. If the stars will eventually all be burned up, then they would already be burned up if they had an infinite amount of time to burn (there is no such thing as a perpetual motion machine). (2) The Law of Redshifts. Hubble discovered that the further away you look in the universe the faster objects appear to be moving away from each other; this is because we are actually looking back in time. What we see took several light years to get here, so we are seeing in the past. Technically speaking, the Big Bang is not a giant explosion like a bomb blast that would just produce chaos. Ross corrects this misnomer stating, "In truth, this 'bang' represents an immensely powerful yet careful planned and controlled release of matter, energy, space, and time within the strict confines of carefully fine-tuned physical constants and laws that govern their behavior and interactions."[8] It was an intricately designed phenomena. (3) Background radiation. Physicists predicted that if the Big Bang took place, there should be a background radiation (i.e., heat). The COBE satellite was able to make accurate measures of 3 degrees centigrade above absolute zero. Ross correctly notes, "Only a hot big bang could account for such a huge specific entropy."[9] He goes on to say, "Moreover, if the specific entropy were any greater or any less, stars and planets would never have existed at any time in the universe's history."[10] Most scientists today and the general public, the people we are trying to reach, the

---

[8] Ibid., 29.
[9] Ibid., 38.
[10] Ibid.

atheists and other unbelievers, all believe in a Big Bang for the reasons stated above. Their own theory proves the universe had a beginning. Something outside the universe had to Bang it into existence. All theories that try to explain this dilemma in a materialist fashion fail. I encourage you to check out Hugh Ross's book *The Creator and the Cosmos* for detailed refutation of the steady state, oscillating universe and multiverse theories held by some who just refuse to admit the obvious deduction from the evidence of a Big Bang—the universe is temporally finite, demanding a non-physical Being who created it out of nothing: God.[11]

The cosmological argument reveals that the best explanation for a finite universe is that something outside the universe, infinite in itself caused the universe. But what can we know about this uncaused cause? Here are some of the things we can know about this supreme being from the evidence:

1. God is self-existent (uncaused). John 5:26. The first cause must be uncaused.
2. God is eternal. Deuteronomy 33:27. The first cause must be eternal.
3. God is independent of anything else (non-contingent, necessary). Psalm 50:9–13, 21; Isaiah 66:1–2. The first cause cannot be contingent.
4. God is all-powerful. Jeremiah 32:17. The first cause must at least be extremely powerful, if not omnipotent.
5. God is personal. Exodus 3:14. The effect cannot be greater than the cause. Power and intelligence are needed. We will see this in the next argument.

One could try to argue against these conclusions about the supreme being, but it seems that each one is the more likely candidate than its alternative. If we are just looking at what is the most

---

[11] See Paul Copan and William Lane Craig, editors, *Contending with Christianity's Critics* (Nashville: B and H Publishing, 2009), chapter 2 for a detailed critique of the multiverse theory.

likely explanation for the universe it would appear that a supreme being that fits the characteristics of the God of the Bible is our best bet, unless you really just don't want to believe. The evidence we have looked at also rules out a few candidates for supreme being. The Hindu and Buddhist view that the universe is God (Pantheism) cannot be true if the universe had a beginning. Tribal and ancestral religions are also negated by the summary above. The only real candidates still standing are Christianity, Judaism, and Islam. Let's now look at the second argument for a supreme being.

The Teleological Argument

The second powerful argument is called the teleological argument for the existence of God. The teleological argument states that the universe appears to have been designed, which demands an intelligent designer. That intelligent designer is the all-knowing God. The universe looks like a giant machine, and we all know that machines were designed. Life is way too complex to have come from an accident; therefore, it probably came from an intelligent designer. A Grand Artist responsible for it best explains the beauty in the world. Can chance alone really explain the fact that we are examining our own self-existence? The universe has stamped all over it "made by an intelligent designer."

Here is the teleological argument in inductive form:

1. The universe appears to have design and purpose.
2. The best explanation for design and purpose is an intelligent designer.
3. Therefore the universe is probably the result of an intelligent designer.
4. That intelligent designer is God.

We have already seen that the universe had a beginning. It could not have started itself. So what is the explanation? Some have suggested that it was started by some other unintelligent cause, but with the teleological argument, we see that it is more likely that the cause of the universe was intelligent and personal. William Paley was one of the first to elaborate on this argument in his famous watchmaker illustration. I would like to present this illustration with my own additions. Imagine you have won a trip to the most remote part of Alaska, where no human being has ever been to before. You are very excited! They drop you off by helicopter, and you are left in a wilderness that is completely pristine. You get out your compass and GPS because there are no human paths. You begin your walk, and all of a sudden, you look down, and lying on the ground is a wristwatch. Your first thought is, *Wow, this is incredible! This must have just formed here by chance. First, perhaps there was volcanic activity that produced the metal in this particular shape. And then an animal must have died next to the metal, and lightning struck it in such a way that this leather band became attached to the metal. It's amazing how all this came about by chance, even in such a way that the watch has the correct time!* No, you would not think that. You would say, "Man, what a bummer! I'm not the first person to be here." The

Designed or Naturally Caused?

intricacy, functionality, purpose, and timing of the event of the watch appearing demands an intelligent designer. A watch demands a watchmaker. But the

Designed or Naturally Caused?

universe is far more complex than the watch and therefore also demands an intelligent designer, especially when you bring human beings into the equation.

How do normal people determine intelligent design in the world? For instance, how do we know if Mount Rushmore came about by chance or design? For most people, common sense tells them wind and water did not form presidents that look like Washington, Jefferson, Lincoln, and Roosevelt. It's possible, but not likely. Let's compare Mount Rushmore to another site in Colorado Springs called the Garden of the Gods. This place is beautiful and includes what is affectionately called the kissing camels. Actually, when you look at the rock formation, it looks more like a cow kissing a camel, but you get the idea. It is beautiful, but it is clearly naturally made by the wind and rain. What is the difference between the kissing camels and Mount Rushmore? Four factors reveal that one is intelligently designed and the other is naturally designed:

1. Purpose: How do we tell the difference between an ink spill and a writer's manuscript? Both have ink applied to paper in one of innumerable possible ways, but the difference is in detected purpose. Scientists have proposed what is called the anthropic principle to explain the universe. The anthropic principle is simply that the universe seems to have been made for humans designed for the purpose of our existence. In *The Creation Hypothesis*, Hugh Ross lists twenty-five design parameters that give evidence for the fine tuning of the universe including the strong nuclear force constant, the gravitational force constant, the ratio of electron to proton mass, the electromagnetic force constant, the velocity of light, etc. This is heavy science stuff, but what it reveals is that there are so many variables in the universe that even if one of the variables was slightly off, there would be no chance of life at all. This is true for the universe in general, our planet in particular, and the existence of human beings. Ross describes one of the necessary constants:

    For example, the mass density of the universe determines how efficiently nuclear fusion operates in the cosmos… If the mass density were too great, too much deuterium (a heavy isotope of hydrogen with one proton and one neutron in the nucleus) would be made in the first few minutes of the universe's existence. This extra deuterium will cause all the stars to burn much too quickly and erratically for any of them to support a planet with life upon it. On the other hand, if the mass density were too small, so little deuterium and helium would be made in the first few minutes that the heavier elements necessary for life would never form in the stars. What this means is that the approximately 100 billion trillion stars we observe in the universe, no more and no fewer, are needed for life to be possible in the universe. Evidently God cared so much for living creatures that he constructed 100 billion trillion stars and carefully crafted them throughout the age of the universe so that at this brief moment in the history of the cosmos humans could exist and have a pleasant place to live. Of all the gods of the various religions of the world, only the God of the Bible is revealed as investing this much (and more) in humanity.[12]

Atheists decry that though the universe is complex and could have been different by any numerable different ways, by chance, we happen to have this one; otherwise, we wouldn't be observing this now. Chance is the god of the gaps for atheists. It is like someone saying a car must have come by chance because every aspect of the automobile can be explained by the laws of physics and chemistry. This is true, but the existence of the car is better explained by an automobile

---

[12] J.P. Moreland, editor, *The Creation Hypothesis* (Downers Grove: IVP, 1994), 164. For a much more detailed explanation see Hugh Ross *The Creator and the Cosmos*, especially chapter 15.

designer and manufacturer.[13] Commonsense people don't grasp for straws in thin air to try to come up with an alternate explanation for the obvious—the universe was designed.

2. Functionality or aesthetics: This second aspect of how we determine whether something is designed by intelligence or by nature goes along with the first aspect of purpose. The purpose is either to fulfill some function or simply for art's sake. The universe displays both functionality and aesthetics. Can we explain beauty any other way than the product of an Artist? Jean Anouilh says, "Beauty is a rare miracle that reduces to silence our doubts about God." Donald Williams says, "Not even the hardest of hearts can see a blazing sunset over the Pacific without some sense of awe."[14]

3. Information-rich intricacy: The difference between the kissing camels and Mount Rushmore is not only purpose, but it is also intricacy. Mount Rushmore is too detailed to be explained by chance. It is possible that wind and rain could create Mount Rushmore by chance, but it is highly improbable because of the detail that reveals (gives information) what four of the USA presidents look like. The universe itself is far more complex than Mount Rushmore. Biological forms are extremely complex and beyond the chance card. Clark Pinnock gives the brain as an illustration:

Consider the human brain, for example. It consists of about three pounds of grey matter, and yet no manmade computer of any size can duplicate the myriad of operations it routinely performs for us every day. Composed of thirty billion nerve cells, the brain is a vast, largely unexplored

---

[13] William Dembski, editor, *Mere Creation* (Downers Grove: IVP, 1998), 34.

[14] Donald Williams, *The Communicators Commentary: Volume 13* (Waco: Word Books, 1986), 150.

continent—one of the wonders of the universe. How can a person be expected to believe that an organ of such incredible complexity and versatility came to exist by accident as the result of an unintelligent and purely material process?[15]

An encyclopedia is an example of the "Duh factor." All the words are combined in such an intricate way that it gives information to us and makes us go "Duh" at the question as to whether we think the encyclopedia was a product of intelligent design. The human brain is far more complex, with an incredibly larger amount of information than an encyclopedia, and the universe is also far more complex than an encyclopedia. Some will appeal to evolution, but this doesn't explain the nonbiological intricacy of the universe (we will get to evolution soon).

4. Timing: If you were eating a bowl of alphabet soup (I don't think they make it anymore, so this illustration only helps old people like me), and the letters *C*, *A*, and *T* floated together, you would think it was a coincidence. But if you had a swimming pool full of alphabet soup and Shakespeare's *Hamlet* appeared, you would suspect a designer. The intricacy combined with the timing would make it very unlikely that chance was responsible, unless the person involved was named Chance. If you saw a sign made of boulders right at the border of Canada and the USA saying "Welcome to Canada," you would not think that they just happened to roll there by chance, because the sign contains too much detailed information combined with taking place at the exact time and space that it did.

When we observe the universe and notice the purpose (Anthropic principle), functionality/aesthetics, information-rich intricacy, and special timing that brings it all together, the most likely explanation

---

[15] Clark Pinnock, *Reason Enough* (Downers Grove: IVP, 1980), 59.

for both the universe and biological organisms such as human life are best explained by some sort of intelligent designer. If it looks like a duck and quacks like a duck and feels like a duck, it is probably a duck (do you want to buy a duck? is an inside joke with my family). Cicero said, "If you saw a splendid house, you surely would not assume that it was built by mice or weasels. A splendid house implies a splendid architect; and a wonderful world implies a divine creator."

I debated atheist Dan Barker in Colorado Springs in July of AD 2000. It was a kick. The local atheist club called Freedom from Religion sponsored the debate and flew in Barker from Chicago. My friends asked if I was afraid that he might stump me. I said, "Why should I be afraid when we have the truth?" He appeared to be similar to the Wizard of Oz, a lot of smoke and mirrors but no substance. The Freedom from Religion newspaper printed a review of the debate and called it a draw. I figured if the atheists said it was a draw, then that means I won. Many of the Christians who attended (it was about three-fourths atheist and one-fourth Christian attendance) came up to me after the debate and said their faith was stronger than ever. One of the things Barker said was that the design argument was based on ignorance rather than facts. I replied, "No, it is based on observation." Listen to what Stephen Meyer says:

> Intelligent agents have unique causal powers that nature does not. When we observe effects that we know only agents can produce, we rightly infer the antecedent presence of a prior intelligence even if we did not observe the action of the particular agent responsible... Brute matter—whether acting randomly or by necessity—does not have the capability to produce information-intensive systems or sequencing. Yet it is not correct to say that we do not know how information arises. We know from experience that intelligent agents create information all the time... Moreover, citing the activity of an intelligent agent really does explain the origin of certain features such as, for

example, the faces on Mount Rushmore or the inscriptions on the Rosetta Stone. (Imagine the absurdity of an archeologist who refused to infer an intelligent cause for the inscriptions on the Rosetta Stone because such an inference would constitute a scribe-of-the gaps fallacy.)[16]

Scientific evidence reveals a beginning to the universe and design throughout. Any idea such as that of atheism is a blind leap into the dark without any evidence and all evidence pointing to the contrary. I do admire their faith.

Evolution and the Teleological Argument

Many have appealed to evolution as a solution to apparent design. Richard Dawkins titled his book *The Blind Watchmaker*, insinuating that evolution working on blind chance is the real cause of the apparent design. First, we must state that at the very most, evolution could be an answer to biological design, but as we have seen, the universe is very complex and acts as a giant machine, demanding a Designer to explain its origin. But evolution is a sinking ship that we don't want to jump on. At the time of Darwin, when scientists thought a cell was just a kind of blob with a basic structure, atheists finally felt at ease with an explanation for the apparent design. Prior to Darwin, the philosophically respectable position was deism. Deists admitted there had to be a god to explain the order of the universe and the complexity of humanity, but they rejected the God of the Bible and the Bible's miraculous claims that seemed to go against the laws of nature. When Darwin suggested an alternative to design for biological complexity, the deists and closet atheists came out of the closet and felt vindicated in their desire to be free of the constraints of a deity. But science has come a long way since Darwin, unearthing a lot of evidence that is embarrassing to Darwinian evolution. We need to differentiate between macroevolution and microevolution to

---

[16] William Dembski, editor, *Mere Creation*, 138–139.

make sure we are talking about the same thing. Everyone believes in microevolution, which is the idea that change takes place within a species (e.g., Humans are getting taller; Finches' beaks can get smaller or larger). Macroevolution, which is what is in question, is the idea that one species can gradually change into a new species and that every living thing on the planet has a common ancestor. Let's look at several problems with evolution, which pulls the rug out from under the satisfied atheists and their blind watchmaker.

The first insurmountable problem with evolution concerns the origin of life. Atheists tell us it all started with a primordial soup. In prehistoric times, there was a pond that had all the necessary ingredients for life, and when lightning struck—*pow!* Life emerged. There are a few difficulties with this scenario. The complexity of life, even of the simplest organism, is far more complex than an entire encyclopedia, so the pond myth (I call it a myth because there is absolutely no evidence for such a pond) would be similar to taking all the letters of an encyclopedia and putting them in a bag and then pouring out the encyclopedia (no spelling errors allowed). A very simple experiment could be done to prove this pond hypothesis: Take a live bug and then squash it. Pick up all the material and put it in a Petri dish and zap it with lightning to see if it comes to life. All the components necessary for life are there because it was just alive, so it should be very simple, right? Guess what? The bugs never come back to life.

The reason the bug experiment doesn't work is due to the verified fact that all scientists know that spontaneous generation is impossible. In most introductions to biology textbooks, there is a chapter at the beginning explaining that life can only produce life. Louis Pasteur proved that rotten meat doesn't produce maggots by enclosing the meat, which keeps the flies from laying their eggs in the rotten meat. All scientists accept the fact that spontaneous generation goes contrary to the evidence and reject it, except in the case of the origin of life, where their theory demands it. In chapter one of their textbooks, they reject the idea of nonliving matter bringing about life, and then in chapter four, they introduce evolution, which contradicts chapter one's findings. They are asking us to reject the scientifically sound theory that only life can produce life and expect us to believe that in the origin of life, there has to be an exception. They are asking us to believe in science fiction, not science without a shred of evidence. We know that only life produces life; therefore, the most likely explanation of the first life is that of an intelligent designer who is alive. Dick Fischer, a theistic evolutionist, says the following statement:

> At this juncture, no scientist has presented even a token amount of credible evidence that a universe can spring into existence unassisted; or that life can come about spontaneously from a chemical soup; or that a DNA molecule, the genetic code of life, can become increasingly complex through time entirely by accident, even if some try to persuade us in those directions.[17]

So how do evolutionists answer this perplexity? Chance! The religion of the atheist is scene in their worship of the god of chance.

Do you remember the Kalam argument I suggested when I covered the cosmological argument? Let's bring it back to the discussion here. We will call it the bio kalam argument:

1. Life cannot be produced from nonlife.
2. Physical life has not existed forever.
3. Therefore, nonphysical life must have created it.

The first problem with evolution is insurmountable. They cannot even get the argument started. We will now see why they cannot sustain the argument either.

The second problem with evolution is that it seems to go against the second law of thermodynamics. If everything tends toward disorder, how can we explain the amazing order? Ravi Zacharias asks the simple question, "How do biological systems climb the ladder of

---

[17] Dick Fischer, "The Origin Solution" Internet, Introduction, 2.

intricacy and order, while the natural world descends to entropy and disorder?"[18] He then explains the gravity of the question:

> A fundamental law of biology must operate in direct opposition to a fundamental law of physics. Scientists argue that the law for the whole does not apply to all of its parts. (This sleight of hand is fraught with serious problems for those who wish to live by their laws.)[19]

It makes sense that if a divine Creator creates and sustains a universe, life could exist alongside the second law, but if chance is all we have, then I don't give it much of a chance.

The third problem with evolution is the embarrassing fossil evidence. Darwin taught us that through natural selection, living forms gradually became more and more complex. If this were true, we should expect to see a gradual progression in the fossil records, but we don't. Darwin himself recognized this problem but was sure that it would be resolved with further research. It has been over 150 years, and we still don't have the fossils. What we actually have verifies the biblical account of instantaneous creation. The Cambrian Explosion uproots the tree of Darwinism.[20]

The Cambrian geologic period began about 540 million years ago according to geologic scientists, and within about three to ten million years most of the phyla around today appeared suddenly (millions of years doesn't sound sudden, but it is just a blip in the geologic record). Lee Strobel puts the problem into perspective:

> "Okay," he said, "imagine yourself on one goal line of a football field. That line represents the first fossil, a microscopic, single-celled organism. Now start marching down the field. You pass the

---

[18] Ravi Zacharias, *A Shattered Visage: The Real Face of Atheism* (Grand Rapids: Baker Books, 1990), 40.

[19] Ibid., 41.

[20] Lee Strobel, *The Case for the Creator* (Grand Rapids: Zondervan, 2004), 45.

twenty-yard line, the forty-yard line, you pass midfield, and you're approaching the other goal line. All you've seen this entire time are these microscopic, single-celled organisms. You come to the sixteen-yard line on the far end of the field, and now you see these sponges and maybe some jellyfish and worms. Then—*boom!*—in the space of a single stride, all these other forms of animals suddenly appear. As one evolutionary scientist said, the major animal groups 'appear in the fossil record as Athena did from the head of Zeus—full blown and raring to go.'[21]

The fossil record presents a huge problem for the evolutionist. Some of the evolutionists themselves admit this difficulty. Here is what evolutionist Stephen Gould admits about the paucity of fossil evidence:

The history of most fossil species includes two features particularly inconsistent with gradualism:

1. Stasis. Most species exhibit no directional change during their tenure on earth. They appear in the fossil record looking pretty much the same as when they disappear; morphological change is usually limited and directionless.
2. Sudden appearance. In any local area, a species does not arise gradually by the steady transformation of its ancestors; it appears all at once and "fully formed."[22]

Both stasis and sudden appearance are the exact opposite of what Darwin predicted would be found in the fossil record. Richard Goldschmidt of the University of California, Berkley, and others

---

[21] Ibid., 44. See Hugh Ross, *The Improbable Planet* (Baker Books: Grand Rapids, 2016) 177 for quotes from leading evolutionary biologists who are not Christians but are in agreement.

[22] Quoted in Phillip Johnson, *Darwin On Trial* (Downers Grove: IVP, 1991), 50.

argued for punctuated equilibrium or saltations also called hopeful monsters similar to the X-Men. This is the idea that an animal could have a baby that has a brand-new, fully developed organ that the mother didn't have. These evolutionists may not put it this bluntly, but in essence, that is what we have because of the shortness of time found in the fossil records. They realized three things: (1) The earth was not in existence long enough for such a slow process as Darwinian evolution or its modern adaptations. (2) Unless the mutation was complete, it would not help to further the reproductive chances of the animal; in fact, it would hinder it. For example, an animal that slowly evolves wings from appendages would become awkward for climbing or grasping and would therefore be easy prey for predators and selected out. In order for a mutation of wings to be an advantage, it would have to evolve in one step from the mother having legs to the baby having wings completely capable of flight. Another example is the eye. An eye would be worthless until the animal had the total complexity of a working eye along with the mental and neural capacity to use the information obtained by the eye. It sounds more like sci-fi or even more like a miracle, but without a miracle worker. (3) There is a total lack of fossil evidence for long term Darwinian evolution. It seems that Gould, Goldschmidt, and others will appeal to anything but the most obvious solution to the fossil dilemma: God created each species through sudden creation, not gradual evolution. Why fight the fossil evidence?

The fourth problem with evolution is that mutations never add information. The modified view commonly held today is that evolution takes place through helpful genetic mutations. First of all, mutations are rarely helpful; they are almost entirely either neutral or hazardous to the animal. Second, mutations only scramble the information already available; they have no ability to add new information.[23]

---

[23] Dr. J.C. Sanford states, "Yet I am still not convinced there is a single, crystal-clear example of a known mutation which unambiguously *created* information." *Genetic Entropy and the Mystery of the Genome* (Lima, New York: Elim Publishing, 2005), 17.

The fifth problem with evolution is the incredible creatures on our planet that defy evolution. Evolutionists say that it is possible that these creatures came around by chance, but we just don't know how. I think the more likely explanation for these incredible creatures is sudden creation by the great artist we call God. Phillip Johnson gives the peacock as an example of natural selection gone awry. The male peacock has a gaudy fan that is an obvious encumbrance when trying to flee a predator. Normally, the peacock would have been selected out by Darwinian standards, except that the peahen is drawn to the large fan, which gives the peacock an advantage for producing offspring, even if it decreases life expectancy. The evolutionist is probably pleased with herself at this point, except she really needs to rethink this problem. Johnson explains below:

> What I find intriguing is that Darwinists are not troubled by the unfitness of the peahen's sexual taste. Why would natural selection, which supposedly formed all birds from lowly predecessors, produce a species whose females lust for males with life-threatening decorations? The peahen ought to have developed a preference for males with sharp talons and mighty wings... It seems to me that the peacock and peahen are just the kind of creatures a whimsical Creator might favor, but that an "uncaring mechanical process" like natural selection would never permit to develop.[24]

Another example given by Rubel Shelly is the amazing bombardier beetle:

> One of my favorite examples of a case in nature that is intelligible in the case of supernatural design and otherwise absurd involves an insect. *Brachinus*, better known as the bombardier bee-

---

[24] Phillip Johnson, *Darwin on Trial*, 30–31.

tle, squirts a lethal mixture of two chemicals into the face of its enemy. When the two chemicals mix, they explode. In order to store those two chemicals in its own body until needed for self-defense, a chemical inhibitor is there to make them harmless. At the instant the beetle squirts the stored liquid from its tail, an anti-inhibitor is added to make the mixture explosive again. The slightest alteration in the chemical balance involved here would result in a race of exploded beetles in only one generation. How reasonable is it to put this complex process down to a lucky roll of the dice as opposed to creative design?[25]

Many other examples could be given, such as the giraffe, but I think you get the point. There are many animals that defy evolution as an explanation for their origin but fit perfectly the idea that an artistic creator and designer brought them into existence.

The sixth problem with evolution is the concept of irreducible complexity. If it can be shown that there are examples of life that are irreducibly complex, meaning all of its parts are necessary for it to function, then evolution could not have brought it about. Michael Behe wrote *Darwin's Black Box* to explain this argument. He gives the mousetrap as an example. If you take away any part of the mousetrap, it could not function; it is irreducibly complex and therefore is a product of a designer. Most people agree that mousetraps are designed rather than evolved from lower species of rodent killers. But if we can find an example in biology of an irreducibly complex living organism, it would disprove macroevolution. Darwin himself admitted that if an irreducibly complex organism could be found, his theory would be disproven. Behe gives the example of the bacterial flagellum. This bacterium has a propeller that spins at ten thousand revolutions per minute and can stop spinning within a quarter turn

---

[25] Rubel Shelly, *Prepare to Answer: A Defense of the Christian Faith* (Grand Rapids: Baker Book House, 1990), 72–73.

and begin spinning the other way at the same speed. He states, "At the bare minimum you need at least three parts—a paddle, a rotor, and a motor—that are made up of various proteins." Without all these intact we would not have a functional flagellum at all.[26] The flagellum is irreducibly complex. Evolutionists can give unproven possibilities to show that it is not irreducibly complex after all, but why not accept what seems to be obvious? The bacterial flagellum was designed.

The seventh problem with evolution is the icons of evolution. Jonathan Wells wrote the book *Icons of Evolution: Science or Myth?* illustrating ten examples used by evolutionists to prove evolution that have actually been disproven by evolutionists themselves, even though they still use them as arguments.[27] Let me briefly describe his findings: (1) The Miller-Urey experiment that supposedly produced life in a lab didn't. There was no life. The experiment used the wrong environment, and intelligence was necessary to produce the experiment. (2) Darwin's tree of life looks more like a field of grass than a tree when the actual fossils are reviewed. (3) Homology in vertebrate limbs is an example of circular reasoning. (4) Haeckel's embryos were fake, and the earliest stages are very dissimilar. (5) Archaeopteryx is not the ancestor of birds. (6) Peppered moths were staged photos. (7) Darwin's finches had no long-term change. (8) Four-winged fruit flies are mutants that die. (9) The horse evolution ends up being a philosophical sleight of hand rather than an actual argument. (10) The ape to human picture is purely hypothetical, arranging pictures to get people to see what they want to see. All the icons are put to the test of the myth busters and found wanting. The strongest argument of the evolutionist for common descent is the concept of shared anatomical features, homology. Why do the hominids look so similar to humans? Fazala Rana states that the shared anatomical features "could just as easily reflect the handiwork of a Creator who chose to employ a common blueprint and reuse many of the same

---

[26] Michael Behe, *Darwin's Black Box* (New York: The Free Press, 1996), 70–72.

[27] Jonathan Wells, *Icons of Evolution: Science or Myth?* (Washington DC: Regnery Publishing, 2000).

design elements."[28] Rana goes on to point out the lack of transitional species for the hominids, and therefore the evolution tree looks more like a lawn when the fossils are evaluated.[29] Why won't the naturalists go where the evidence points? It is because their worldview won't let them, not because they are following the evidence. Commonsense people go with the evidence.

Why, when all the facts are reviewed, do so many intelligent people hold on to something so contrary to the evidence? I believe it is because they can't conceive of any viable alternative. I am not claiming that just because evolution is inconceivable, that proves there must be a god. All I am trying to do here is break down an idol of the secularist so that he or she might view the evidence for the existence of God with an open mind.

It is suggested that through chance mutations that are beneficial to an organism, survival of the fittest takes over, and so life evolves, in a sense suspending the second law of thermodynamics. Darwin expected the fossil evidence to back him up. It did not. In the fossil records, species appear suddenly, and due to catastrophes, they disappear suddenly. Darwinian evolution demands gradual change. There is no fossil evidence for this, and it doesn't make sense. Other evolutionary schemes run into other problems as suggested above. The gradual change would actually be detrimental to the species until it has a fully functioning new organ. Survival of the fittest would select it out before it ever evolved. The fossil evidence goes against evolution. Once again, one can take a blind leap in the dark and believe it anyway, but it is not reasonable. The blind gambles atheists make in accepting all this show their tremendous faith, but I would not recommend they go to Las Vegas.

Here is the teleological argument:

1. The universe appears to have design and purpose.

---

[28] Fazala Rana with Hugh Ross, Who Was Adam? (RTB Press: Covina, CA, 2015), 144.
[29] Ibid., chapter 9.

2. The best explanation for design and purpose is an intelligent designer.
3. Therefore, the universe is probably the result of an intelligent designer.

An intelligent designer would be intelligent, wise, personal, alive, creative, and appreciative of beauty. This intelligent designer perfectly fits the God of the Bible.

The Moral Argument

The third commanding evidence is called the moral argument for the existence of God. It states that if there is a universal moral code, there must be a universal moral code giver. Everyone has a conscience and knows that certain things are right and wrong. When we are wronged, we demand justice and expect the wrongdoer to agree that he or she was wrong. We appeal to a universal moral code. "Hitler was wrong" is not just my opinion. It is absolutely true, and Hitler should have known it, which is why we held him accountable for his actions. This universal moral code giver is the all-loving God. Here it is stated in logical form:

1. There appears to be a universal moral code.
2. A universal moral code seems to demand a universal lawgiver.
3. Therefore, there probably is a universal lawgiver.
4. The universal lawgiver is God.

Three questions need to be addressed: (1) Is there a universal moral code? In other words, are there moral absolutes? (2) Does a universal moral code demand a code giver? (3) What is the code giver like?

First, are there moral absolutes? C. S. Lewis makes two observations:

> First, that human beings, all over the earth, have this curious idea that they ought to behave in a certain way, and cannot really get rid of it. Secondly, that they do not in fact behave in that way. They know the Law of Nature; they break it. These two facts are the foundation of all clear thinking about ourselves and the universe we live in.[30]

No matter where you go or what society or culture you study, the same basic moral laws seem to be assumed, like don't murder, don't steal, don't lie, be fair. Of course, there are differences among the various cultures that have existed in our world, and there are grey areas. Paul Copan argues, "Just because moral uncertainty or ambiguity exists, this doesn't eclipse the morally obvious. As Dr. Samuel Johnson put it, 'The fact that there is such a thing as twilight does not mean that we cannot distinguish between day and night.'"[31] We all know there is right and wrong and that we sometimes do wrong even though we know it is wrong. Where did this idea of right and wrong come from? It is true for society, and it is true of the individual.

We all have a conscience. We are compelled to do certain things even though we don't want to, often when it goes directly against our natural instincts. We feel we *ought* to do something or we *ought* to abstain from something else. There appears to be a law within us, a sense of ought. If we steal from someone, we may feel guilty, or we may attempt to justify our actions in this particular situation (he is rich and doesn't deserve this), but we all know deep down that stealing is wrong. When someone steals from us, we complain. We don't complain simply because we were inconvenienced. We appeal to a

---

[30] C. S. Lewis, *Mere Christianity* (New York: Harper Collins, 2001), 8.

[31] Francis Beckwith, editor, *To Everyone an Answer* (Downers Grove: IVP, 2004), 111.

universal code: "You were wrong to steal from me." Even if the thief doesn't agree, you believe he or she should have known better and should not have stolen. We all have a conscience, and so we appeal to the other person's conscience.

Some reject objectively binding moral obligations in favor of what is called cultural relativism. Cultural relativism is the idea that there are no moral absolutes; all morals come from our upbringing in the particular society we grow up in and the circumstances we live through. What might be right for me may not be right for you, and what might be evil for you may be good for me. Many point out the dissimilarities of ethical standards in different cultures to back up this view. In actuality, the amazing thing is the abundant similarities of basic moral values among all cultures. The most serious problem with moral relativism is that it nullifies any possibility for moral progress. If there is no real standard, then to say we are better or worse now is senseless. We cannot condemn those who promote antisemitism, racism, or infanticide. To speak out against a culture would go against cultural relativism. Besides the vast similarities of ethics in the various cultures and the fact that cultural relativism does away with any possibility of moral progress, nobody lives by this idea in day-to-day practice. To say you believe something is true and yet all your life is lived as if it were not true is to deny that you really believe it is true (except when convenient). C. Stephen Evans explains this:

> It is extremely difficult to hold consistently to any form of relativism or emotivism in practice. It is easy enough to say that there are no real moral obligations; but most people cannot help believing that, when they are wronged by someone else, the act is really wrong. If a person maliciously trips me and then laughs because I have cut my lip, it will seem to me that the person has wronged me and that it is a true fact that he has done so. It is no good to say that the person who tripped me thought the act was right and

therefore for him it was right. The act was wrong, and the person should have recognized this and regretted the act, even if he felt no such emotion. The person who did the tripping is likely to say the same thing when *he* is tripped.[32]

Jesus taught, "Just as you want others to do for you, do the same for them" (Luke 6:31). Is this statement a universal moral law? I would go so far as to say that it is a self-evident truth. Everyone knows it is true, and everyone wants everyone else to live by it. Take slavery for instance. Many societies have approved of slavery, but who in their right mind would say it was good that someone forced them to be a slave?

There seems to be a universal moral code with moral absolutes. We all live as if this is true. We all sense that certain things are right or wrong. We all have a conscience. If relativism is true, then there is no place for progress. These ideas are based on observation and pragmatism. Pragmatism doesn't prove something is true, but it does cause us to think seriously about the alternatives. The most likely explanation for the apparent universal moral code is that there is a universal moral code.

But then our second question needs to be answered: Does a universal moral code demand a code giver? Peter Kreeft gives a compelling argument for the affirmative, so allow me to quote his reasoning in its entirety:

> Isn't it remarkable that no one, even the most consistent subjectivist, believes that it is ever good for anyone to deliberately and knowingly disobey his or her own conscience? Even if different people's consciences tell them to do or avoid totally different things, there remains one moral absolute for everyone: never disobey your own conscience. Now where did conscience get

---

[32] C. Stephen Evans, *Philosophy of Religion* (Downers Grove: IVP, 1982), 71.

such an absolute authority—an authority admitted even by the moral subjectivist and relativist? There are only four possibilities.

1. From something less than me (nature)
2. From me (individual)
3. From others equal to me (society)
4. From something above me (God)

Let's consider each of these possibilities in order.

1. How can I be absolutely obligated by something less than me—for example, by animal instinct or practical need for material survival?
2. How can I obligate myself absolutely? Am I absolute? Do I have the right to demand absolute obedience from anyone, even myself? And if I am the one who locked myself in this prison of obligation, I can also let myself out, thus destroying the absoluteness of the obligation, which we admitted as our premise.
3. How can society obligate me? What right do my equals have to impose their values on me? Does quantity make quality? Do a million human beings make a relative into an absolute? Is "society" God?
4. The only source of absolute moral obligation left is something superior to me. This binds my will, morally, with rightful demands for complete obedience.

Thus God, or something like God, is the only adequate source and ground for the absolute moral obligation we all feel to obey our conscience. Conscience is thus explainable only as the voice

of God in the soul. The Ten Commandments are
ten divine footprints in our psychic sand.[33]

In the United States, we have moved from a Judeo-Christian
set of moral values to an "anything goes" code. The moral landscape
is changing rapidly because there is no moral foundation left after
God is jettisoned from the equation. We have our moral feet firmly
planted in midair, yet we all know deep down that there is a right and
a wrong. Where did that knowledge come from? Where do moral
absolutes come from?

We have seen that it makes the best sense out of what we can
observe that there is a universal moral code and there are moral absolutes.[34] We have also recognized that the best explanation for a universal moral code is a universal moral code giver. But what is that
code giver like? At the very least, a universal code giver would have
to be personal, in charge, and good. He, she, or it would have to be
personal because an impersonal force could not have morally binding
authority over persons. He, she, or it would have to be in charge of
the universe; otherwise, his, her, or its moral authority would not be
universally binding. He, she, or it would have to be good to be able
to demand that we be good. The God of the Bible fits this description perfectly when properly understood.[35]

Conclusion

These three arguments (cosmological, teleological, and moral) reveal
that it is more intelligent to believe that there is some kind of God
than to think there isn't a God. This God also appears to be powerful,
intelligent, and moral. The intelligent agnostic should become a the-

---

[33] Peter Kreeft and Ronald Tacelli, *Handbook of Christian Apologetics* (Downers
Grove: IVP, 1994), 74–75.

[34] Most would agree to the moral absolutes that it is wrong to steal other people's
babies and it is wrong to murder people just for fun.

[35] Some think God is a moral monster because he advocates slavery and genocide.
For an excellent rebuttal to this accusation see Paul Copan, *Is God a Moral
Monster?* (Ada, MI: Baker Books, 2010).

ist after evaluating these arguments, unless he or she is very stubborn. This evidence doesn't demand the Christian God, but the Christian God does fit the evidence. Let's now turn to the substantiation of Christianity.

A CASE FOR CHRISTIANITY

Theism doesn't go far enough. So far, we have seen that it is not very intelligent to deny God or even to be agnostic about God, but is there any evidence revealing who or what that God is? It seems to be common sense that if there is a supreme being, He would want to reveal Himself in a clear way to humanity, because He is good and would want us to know what we should think about Him and His plan for us. Two fantastic pieces of evidence are available: the Bible and Jesus. Many claim that the Bible is full of myths, has been changed over the years, and is full of errors. Others assert that Jesus is nothing spectacular once the historical Jesus is discovered. Is there a case for Christianity? Let's see.

The Bible Is God's Word[36]

The Bible claims to be God's Word. If it is His Word, then it makes sense that it is trustworthy and reveals the true God. When the Bible is examined, we discover that it is God's Word. Isaiah 41:21–24 says that the true God would be able to describe the past accurately, predict the future in detail without error, and have miracles bearing witness to His authenticity. This is a great test, and the Bible passes all three parts of the test.

---

[36] For an excellent and thorough resource on the supernatural nature of the Bible see my book *The Uniqueness of the Bible* (Bloomington, IN: Westbow Press, 2015).

God Described the Past Accurately

Archaeologists have put the Bible to the test very thoroughly, and it has come through with flying colors. It seems very unlikely that over forty people writing in three different languages on three different continents over a period of fifteen hundred years could have known so accurately what went on before them. Remember they all wrote before the science of archaeology was invented. There are many great books on archaeology, but let me mention two finds that reveal the Bible is reliable and like no other book: Jericho and the Dead Sea Scrolls.

One particular incident is worthy of note because of its more than coincidental nature concerning the recording of the miraculous account of the Hebrews' destruction of the city of Jericho. There is a question of dating the fall of Jericho, which concerns a time period of not more than 150 years, but the facts concerning the destruction fit the biblical account well.[37] Ancient Jericho has been excavated four times, and the basic results show that fire and an earthquake destroyed the city, and an abundance of grain was found on the site. Apparently, invaders attacked the city and were able to get in because the walls had collapsed outward from the earthquake. The aggressors attacked shortly after harvest, as is seen by a plethora of jars of grain found. This is curious because that would be an unconventional time militarily for attack. It is even more interesting that the assailants did not plunder the grain. The account recorded in Joshua states that immediately after Passover (after harvest), the Israelites attacked Jericho, and the walls came down after they shouted. The Israelites then burned the city, leaving everything as an offering to God by God's command. Apart from the discrepancy of dating, "the details

---

[37] For alternative dates of 1550 and 1400 see Piotr Bienkowski, "Jericho Was Destroyed in the Middle Bronze Age, Not the Late Bronze Age," *Biblical Archaeology Review*, 16, no.5 (1990), 45–69 for the 1550 date and Bryant G. Wood, "Did the Israelites Conquer Jericho?" *Biblical Archaeology Review* 16, no.2 (1990), 45–59 for the 1400 date.

surrounding the destruction of Jericho City IV thus closely parallel what we read in the Bible."[38]

The Dead Sea Scrolls are probably the greatest archaeological find in history. We do not have perfect copies of the twenty-four (thirty-nine with the Christian counting method)[39] books of the Old Testament, but when the various manuscripts are compared, few major difficulties remain. The earliest extant Masoretic texts we have are the Codex Cairensis (containing the former and latter prophets dating AD 895), Aleppo Codex (entire Hebrew Bible dating early tenth century) and the Leningrad MS B-19A (entire Hebrew Bible AD 1010). In 1947, the Dead Sea Scrolls (DSS), which date between 250 BC and AD 135, were discovered. The DSS represent various writings from the Qumran community of Essenes, including every book of the Hebrew Bible except Esther. These manuscripts represent various families of texts but are remarkably close to the Masoretic manuscripts. One scroll of Isaiah dated 100 BC and thus a thousand years earlier than the earliest Hebrew manuscript we had prior to the discovery of the DSS, is almost identical to the Masoretic script.[40]

Many people claim that the Bible cannot be trusted because of copying errors. You have heard the illustration of the game of telephone that supposedly proves the Bible wasn't copied accurately. When you whisper into the first person's ear one sentence, then that person whispers the sentence into the next person's ear and so on until it goes around the circle, the last person declares the sentence, which is usually completely different from the original sentence. This

[38] *NIV Archaeology Study Bible* (Grand Rapids: Zondervan, 2005), 312.

[39] Christian Bibles count the books differently and place them in a different order than the Hebrew Bible but include the identical books. Christian Bibles follow the Septuagint order and number of books. The numbering is different because Greek takes up more space than Hebrew because of the vowels and so books like Kings became First and Second Kings. All twelve Minor Prophets are included as one book in the Hebrew Bible.

[40] Mark Norton compares the two texts, "Except for a few instances where spelling and grammar differ between the Dead Sea Scrolls and the Masoretic Text, the two are amazingly similar. The differences do not warrant any major changes in the substance of the Old Testament." Philip Wesley Comfort, editor, *The Origin of the Bible* (Wheaton: Tyndale, 2003), 166.

game has been applied to the Bible, but archaeology has revealed that the end result of the game is not the case for the Bible. The Dead Sea Scrolls were a big help in that discovery. Over a thousand years of copying and yet Isaiah comes out virtually unscathed. It is because of two factors: First, the copyists were not casual game players. They practiced detailed checks and balances to make sure they accurately copied the texts because they valued the texts as God's Word. Second, the Holy Spirit made sure the manuscripts were accurately copied. It makes sense that if God is the ultimate author of the Bible, He would keep it preserved so that we could all be confident in what it says.

Some might argue, "Then why didn't God preserve the original writings?" Think about this question. If we had the originals, Christians would probably have worshiped them, because we are so prone to idolatry. God preserved us from that. Also, if we had the originals, who would be their keeper? If one group controlled the originals, what would keep them from altering them without anyone knowing? If that group became corrupt, they could use them for ill will rather than good, and no one would know the difference. Instead, in God's brilliance, He had the books copied and made sure they were preserved carefully. We have over ten thousand manuscripts of the New Testament. There are differences between the manuscripts, but when they are all studied, an accurate copy can be revealed with very few discrepancies and no theological differences at all. The early church mass copied the letters of the New Testament and sent them all over the Roman Empire, which ensured that no one individual or group could control the letters of the New Testament. God is brilliant!

God Predicted the Future in Detail Without Error

The Bible makes hundreds of predictions of the distant future in precise detail, and everything has come to pass exactly as described (except the prophecies concerning the end of the world because that hasn't happened yet). God is not like Nostradamus who was extremely vague or Jean Dixon who is woefully inaccurate. He predicts the future in detail without error. There are many great prophecies we could discuss, but let me mention two: Tyre and Messiah.

The Bible made several prophecies of the complete destruction of cities. Many of the cities it said would be rebuilt, and several it claimed would never be rebuilt. The Bible is one hundred percent accurate in both categories as archeology shows. One amazing example is the city of Tyre. Ezekiel 26 predicts the following:

1. Nebuchadnezzar will take the city.
2. Other nations will participate in the fulfillment.
3. The city is to be made flat like the top of a rock.
4. It is to become a place for spreading nets.
5. Its stones and timber are to be laid in the sea.
6. The old city of Tyre will never be rebuilt.

History records that Nebuchadnezzar took the city, but the people escaped out to an island. Later, Alexander the Great took the island off the coast by taking the old city's rubble and throwing it into the sea, making a land bridge. This caused the old city to look flat like a rock due to the scraping of the material. The old city is now a place for fisherman, but no city has been planted there, even though there is an excellent water supply to support a major city. Ezekiel's prediction was not fulfilled for hundreds of years, but in the end, the precise detail is observed without error. How could Zeke know Alex was coming hundreds of years later?

The prophecies concerning Messiah make a great case for the uniqueness of the Bible, where the Messiah's birthplace (Micah 5:2), time of ministry (Daniel 9:24–27), miracles (Isaiah 42:1–9), and means of death (Isaiah 53, Zechariah 12:10, Psalm 22 describing crucifixion hundreds of years before it was even invented) were predicted hundreds of years before Jesus, who just happened to fulfill every one of them. The prophecies are miraculous, but the *way* God predicts the Messiah is also astonishing.

Have you ever read a detective novel or watched a show like Colombo, where clues are given throughout the book or show but the mystery isn't discovered until the end? When you go back and reread or watch the mystery, you see all the clues right in front of your face, though clearly hidden until all is revealed. What if God orchestrated His plan in such a manner? If God were to reveal His plan without mystery, Satan would know how to thwart it. What if God, in all His brilliance, actually used His archenemy to accomplish His plans using the tactic of mystery? Rabbi Paul suggests that is exactly what God did (1 Corinthians 2:8). Let's look at how God revealed to Moses, David, Isaiah, and Zechariah His grand plan that duped the devil but became apparent after it was completed (examples from the Torah, Ketuvim, and Nevi'im, the three parts of the Hebrew Scriptures).

Moses. God gave the Torah to Moses. The Torah is good, but people cannot live up to it. Moses even told God's people that they wouldn't be able to keep the law (Deuteronomy 30:1–6; 31:15–18, 29), but he also predicted Messiah would solve our problem of non-Torah keeping (Genesis 49:10; Numbers 24:17). Messiah would be like Moses (Deuteronomy 18:15; 34:10–12; Numbers 12:3–8) seeing God face to face, performing incredible miracles, and bringing a new law and a new covenant (Deuteronomy 30:6; Jeremiah 31:31–34; Ezekiel 36:24–36).

David. David was not perfect, but he was a man after God's heart (1 Samuel 13:14). God made a covenant with him that he would have a descendent on the throne who would reign forever as Messiah King (2 Samuel 7:16; Psalm 89). Every king after him was judged as to how they measured up to David (e.g., 1 Kings 15:3). Many of David's Psalms have been recognized as Messianic Psalms, with an initial reference to David or a king of that time but a more complete fulfillment in Messiah (Psalms 2, 16, 22, 68, 69, 72, 89, 109, 110, 118, 132). God used *typology* to keep the prediction in mystery until its fulfillment. Messiah would reign, but He would also suffer. Psalm 22 presents Him as forsaken by God (1), with all His bones out of joint (14), thirsting (15), pierced in hands and feet (16), clothes divided by casting lots (18), and victorious in the end (22–31), declaring, "It is finished!" As a detective knowing that later the Romans would perfect crucifixion, this description sounds a lot like crucifixion, even though crucifixion had not been invented yet for several hundred years. What was David talking about?

Isaiah. Isaiah is called the prince of the prophets and for good reason. More than any other, he paints the picture of Messiah with striking detail and raw beauty. Isaiah 9:1–7 describes how the government will be on His shoulders, He will even be called "Mighty God," and He will reign on David's throne and over his kingdom forever. Isaiah 11 describes Messiah as the branch who will restore Eden-like conditions to our world, taking care of everyone. Isaiah 42 and 61 detail how Messiah will have a gentle but powerful ministry; He is unique! He is coming as conquering King, but it also appears that He comes as suffering servant (Isaiah 52:13–53:12). Some have suggested that the servant is Israel or ideal Israel, but this figure sounds a lot like the figure described in Psalm 22. He suffers for Israel, so He cannot be Israel, which is why the ancient rabbis understood this to refer to Messiah. Isaiah 53:5 states, "He was pierced for our transgressions, he was crushed for our iniquities; the punishment that brought us peace was on him, and by his wounds we are healed." He is described as a lamb for sacrifice. Could He be the ultimate sacrifice that brings our complete forgiveness, paying the penalty we were supposed to pay for our sins so that we could have a personal relationship with God? Is Messiah the fulfillment of the entire sacrificial system, which is why the temple is no longer needed? It is remarkable that the servant is found alive at the end of the chapter after He experienced the violent death of being pierced and crushed (11–12).

Zechariah. Zechariah was one of the last prophets, exhorting God's people after the return from the exile. His book is filled with mystery and imagination. He describes the very end in chapter 14. In Zechariah 12:10, he reveals in the last days that God's people will have an epiphany. It says, "And I [God] will pour out on the house of David and the inhabitants of Jerusalem a spirit of grace and supplication. They will look on me, the one they have pierced, and they will mourn for him as one mourns for an only child, and grieve bitterly for him as one grieves for a firstborn son." This grief will result in complete cleansing and forgiveness (13:1). It appears that

Zechariah is predicting that God's people, the children of Israel, will have rejected Messiah, God's plan, but will realize their mistake in the end and be saved (Psalm 118:22–23).

Let's put on our detective hats now. Has anyone come in the past who was like Moses, suffered by piercing in hands and feet, and was initially rejected by His own people, but who ended up alive after being killed and promises to come back and reign as king in Jerusalem? I believe all the signs point to Jesus (Yeshua). Jesus of Nazareth was like Moses. He performed incredible miracles that even the unbelieving Jews recognized as miracles, though they claimed it was by Beelzebub. Jesus brought the new law in the Sermon on the Mount, and He brought the new covenant. Jesus had an even more personal relationship with God, not just face to face but Father to Son. Jesus was crucified as described in Psalm 22, Isaiah 53, and Zechariah 12:10, and He rose from the dead, the greatest miracle of all. The book of Hebrews reveals how He is superior to angels, Moses, the old covenant, sacrificial system, and everything else. Jesus is the ultimate revelation of God because He is God, and He is the plan of God.[41]

Miracles Bear Witness to the Bible's Authenticity

Miracles are described throughout the Bible, and the best explanation for their prevalence is that they actually occurred. Unlike other religious books, the Bible is based on historically reliable and testable facts. These things actually happened in space and time. The most amazing miracle and best attested is the resurrection of Jesus; we will examine this miracle in more detail below. There is no other book like the Bible; it is in a class of its own. Archaeology backs up the Bible, but it destroys other religious books' claims to truth. No other religious book has fulfilled prophecy, not even the Qur'an, and so no other religious book can pass the stringent test put out in Isaiah

---

[41] A great resource for prophecies fulfilled among other evidences is Josh McDowell and Sean McDowell, *Evidence That Demands a Verdict* (Nashville: Thomas Nelson, 2017).

41:21–24, but the Bible was not afraid to predict the future in detail because God is its author. The Bible is full of miracles performed by the prophets, including crossing the Red Sea on dry land, raising the dead, healing the sick, and walking on water (I walked across Lake Pepin in Minnesota, but it was frozen at the time). The greatest miracle and miracle worker is Jesus.

Jesus Is God's Word

Jesus is the best proof of all for who God is. The Gospels record eyewitness accounts of Jesus's life, death, and resurrection, which date within thirty years of the events. This is simply not enough time for legend to creep in because the eyewitnesses would have spoken out against any false testimony. We also have several non-Christian first century sources admitting to the basic facts of Jesus's life and death. These sources are important because they are antagonistic to Christianity (both Jewish and Roman).[42] If the opposition agrees with the basic historic facts, then you know it is probably true. Think of it like this: If a republican and a democrat were debating some issue, and the democrat conceded to one of the points of the republican, it would be strong evidence that the republican was correct on that point; otherwise, the democrat would never have conceded. It is the same with the first-century opposition to Jesus. They all basically agreed that there was a man named Jesus who gathered a group of followers, performed miracles (the Jews said He did it by the power of the devil; notice they are admitting that He did miracles), that He was crucified under Pontius Pilate, and that three days later the body was missing (the Jews said the disciples stole the body; notice that they admit that the body was missing).

Jesus is the only one who truly has solved our problem of sin. He died on the cross, paying the penalty we deserved to pay for our

---

[42] For more detailed information see my book, *The Uniqueness of the Bible*, as well as Gary Habermas, *The Historical Jesus: Ancient Evidence for the Life of Christ* (Joplin, MO: College Press, 1996). Roman and Jewish historians such as Tacitus, Suetonius, Josephus, Thallus, Pliny the Younger, etc., all substantiate these basic facts.

sins. God is holy and just and must punish sin, but Jesus has taken that penalty for us as our substitute; He took the wrath of God on himself when He died on the cross. If we repent of our sin and place our faith in Jesus and His finished work on the cross, surrendering to him as Lord, we are saved from all our sins—past, present, and future sin. He was able to do this because He is God. The second person of the Trinity took on a second nature, that of humanity and was born of the Virgin Mary. He lived a perfect life, taught the greatest ethics in the world, performed miracles, died on the cross for our sins, and rose from the dead. Only Christianity adequately solves the most pressing problem of the world.

Jesus proved He is who He said He was (God) by His resurrection.[43] The resurrection is the greatest miracle of all time, and it actually happened. When we consider all the evidence, it is the most logical explanation for the empty tomb. Let us look at the evidence for the resurrection of Jesus. Only the Muslims deny Jesus was crucified, because as we have already seen, the historical records with multiple attestation from both sympathetic and hostile parties are in complete agreement to the basic facts that a man named Jesus gathered a group of followers in Israel and was crucified under Pontius Pilate. There are no claims to the contrary until the seventh century.[44] The only reason anyone would renounce the historical data that substantiates the crucifixion of Jesus is an a priori conviction that it goes against Islamic belief, which must be rejected as willful ignorance. We will now look at the evidence for the missing body and see that the best explanation for the missing body is the resurrection.

---

[43] For a plethora of evidence of the resurrection see Michael Licona, *The Resurrection of Jesus: A New Historiographical Approach* (Downers Grove: IVP Academic, 2010).

[44] Mohammad denied the crucifixion and so does the forgery known as the Gospel of Barnabas, which could not have been written before the fourteenth century. Norman Geisler and Abdul Saleeb, *Answering Islam* (Grand Rapids: Baker, 1993), 295–299. Some confuse the Gospel of Barnabas with the Epistle of Barnabas, which is a legitimate letter written between AD 70 and AD132. The Gospel of Barnabas is never mentioned by anyone in history, including Muslim apologists until the fifteenth century AD. If it existed prior to this, the medieval Muslim apologists would have cited it.

William Lane Craig sums up the evidence "in three independently established facts: (1) Jesus's empty tomb, (2) Jesus's appearances alive after His death, and (3) the origin of the disciples' belief in His resurrection."[45] The empty tomb is substantiated by very early, independent sources. The verses in 1 Corinthians 15:3–5, Acts 13:28–31, and Mark 15:37–16:7 all agree that Jesus died, was buried, was raised, and appeared alive to His followers. Paul wrote 1 Corinthians 15:3–5 no later than the spring of AD 55, but the language indicates "the transmission of a formal early Christian tradition" received by Paul at his conversion around AD 33.[46] This tradition dates within five years of Jesus's death. There is no question that the early church, from its inception, believed Jesus died on the cross and three days later the tomb was empty. There was not enough time for a myth to develop, which is what Liberals and Muslims are suggesting.

The belief of Jesus being raised from the dead is the most logical explanation for the missing body. We must explain the fact that there was no body in the tomb. Let us review the possibilities unbelievers have presented:

1) Some have suggested that the body is still in the tomb; perhaps the disciples went to the wrong tomb. This idea would at least exonerate the disciples from the accusation of deception, but it is highly unlikely they would all forget where their rabbi was placed after the crucifixion. If the body was still in the tomb, then when the Jewish officials saw all the commotion of the Christians claiming Jesus rose from the dead, all they would have to do is say "No, he didn't. Here's his body." But they could not do that because the body was missing. What the Jewish officials actually did was claim that the disciples stole the body. This is the second option.

---

[45] William Lane Craig, *On Guard* (Colorado Springs: David C. Cook, 2010), 219.

[46] James Taylor, *Introducing Apologetics* (Grand Rapids: Baker, 2006), 204-205.

2) The disciples stole the body. The tomb was guarded by soldiers and was blocked by a very heavy boulder with a Roman seal placed on it. Let's just assume that the disciples snuck into the graveyard when the guards just happened to fall asleep (even though it was a death penalty for a guard to fall asleep on duty). They very quietly removed the boulder and stole the body. If this is true, then we must deal with the problem of the credibility and the faithfulness of the disciples. The disciples turned from cowards to lions after the supposed resurrection. Would that have happened if they knew it to be a lie? The disciples are responsible for recording the book with the highest ethical standards known to humankind, which constantly demands truthfulness and condemns lies; is this possible for wicked liars? I say wicked liars because this would mean that they consciously misled people who would later die for that deception. Would these same disciples be willing to die for what they knew to be a lie? If they stole the body when the Romans demanded them to recant, they would have gladly rejected Jesus, knowing He was still a corpse. But they didn't. They all went to their horrible deaths claiming that Jesus rose from the dead and that He changed their lives. A person might be willing to die for something he thought was true when in actuality it is not true, but no one would be willing to die for something that he knew was not true. If the disciples stole the body, then they knew Jesus did not rise from the dead, and they would not have been willing to die for that belief. The idea that the disciples stole the body was the predominant view of the Jews of the first three centuries, which is great evidence that the tomb was empty, but it does not square with the facts.

3) Because of the impossibility of the first two explanations another option was presented in the twentieth century—the swoon theory. This theory states that Jesus did not actually die on the cross. He only appeared dead. When He was placed in the cool tomb, He was resuscitated and then

appeared to the disciples. We still, however, have the problem of His getting by the guards and removing the boulder. We must also assume that the centurion, whose entire job in life was to make sure the criminals were dead, was wrong in this case. Additionally, John would have had to lie about the incident of the soldier piercing Jesus's side after He died because the account says that blood and water came out, which pathologists tell us is proof of death. Not only this, but we must imagine a weak, half-dead Jesus somehow appeared to the disciples in strength and glory enough to convince them that He had risen from the dead. This would make Jesus a liar. I find it amazing that this is even considered as a possible explanation for the missing body. The Muslim view that God swapped Jesus with Judas, having Judas die on the cross as Jesus's lookalike, is another version of the theory that Jesus did not actually die, but it cannot explain the missing body and turns God into a liar. The Bible declares that God cannot lie or deceive (Hebrews 6:18), which is a much more logical understanding of the ethical nature of a perfect supreme being than that of the Qur'an, which declares God deceives (Surah 27:4; 4:143).

Let me suggest one other possibility: Jesus rose from the dead! Unless we have preconceived biases against the possibility of miracles (which is foolish because if God exists, He can certainly do miracles), we must conclude that the most logical explanation for the missing body is that Jesus was raised from the dead. If Jesus was resurrected, then He is Lord, and we had better listen to Him when He says, "I am the way and the truth and the life. No one comes to the Father except through me" (John 14:6).

Not only is the empty tomb evidence for the resurrection, but Jesus's appearances alive after His death is also strong confirmation of the resurrection. The first people to see that the tomb was empty and Jesus was alive were women (Matthew 28:1–10; Mark 16:9; Luke 24:1–11; John 20:1–3, 11–18). In the first century, the testimony of a woman was not credible, so it is quite amazing that all four

Gospels agree that women were the first witnesses of the resurrection. If someone were to make up the story that Jesus rose from the dead and appeared to His followers, he would never have invented the idea that women were the first witnesses because it would not have been believed by the hearers. If this story was made up, the deceiver would have recorded that men were the first to see Jesus alive, perhaps some prominent person. The only reason someone would have written down the idea that Jesus first appeared to women is that He really did appear to them; this is a sound argument unless you are a misogynist. The testimony of all four Gospels is very strong evidence to the fact that Jesus did appear to these women alive after being crucified.

Another verification of Christ's resurrection is the salvation of his brothers. Before Jesus died, His brothers did not believe in Him (Mark 3:21, 31–35; John 7:5). This honest declaration is not the sort of thing deceivers would put into their story, but it is just the sort of thing God would include if it were true. The Bible is unique among religious books in that it describes its heroes truthfully, warts and all, even if that truth might detract from the character's prestige (e.g., David's sin). Jesus did not have any warts, but admitting that His own brothers did not believe in Him might deter some from believing. The fact that the unbelief of Jesus's brothers is recorded gives credence to the historical accuracy of the account. His brothers did not believe in Him while He was alive, but something changed after His death. We know that at least James and Jude became believers after Jesus died, and according to the first century Jewish historian Josephus, James was killed for his faith by the Sanhedrin shortly after AD 60. [47] What caused the dramatic change? In 1 Corinthians 15:7, it says that Jesus appeared to James after His death. William Lane Craig puts this information into perspective:

> Now how is this to be explained? On the one hand, it seems certain that Jesus' brothers did not believe in Him during His lifetime. Jesus' crucifixion would only confirm in James' mind

---

[47] (*Antiquities* 20.200).

that his elder brother's messianic pretensions were delusory, just as he had thought. On the other hand, it's equally certain that Jesus' brothers became ardent Christians, active in ministry. Many of us have brothers. What would it take to make you believe that your brother is the Lord, so that you would die for this belief, as James did? Can there be any doubt that the reason for this remarkable transformation is to be found in the fact that "then he appeared to James"?[48]

Jesus also appeared to Peter and the rest of the apostles, who were in hiding due to cowardice before these appearances and were bold witnesses of the resurrection after these manifestations. The resurrection best explains these turnarounds. The Apostle Paul also claimed to have seen Jesus alive after his death. It is difficult to explain how this man, who at one time zealously pursued the death of Christians, became a Christian after seeing the risen Christ and later died for his faith. Finally, 1 Corinthians 15 states that over five hundred people saw Jesus alive at one time. At the time of the writing, most of the people were still alive and could have been questioned. The pronouncements of the appearances of Christ to so many were recorded so early that it did not leave enough time for myth to develop, because the facts could have been checked out and exposed by the opposition; this is also true of the Gospel accounts themselves. Nineteenth-century liberalism claimed the Gospels were written in the second century, which would have given ample time to develop myth, but the twentieth century has produced a tremendous amount of research and manuscript evidence that contradicts those claims, exposing them to anti-supernatural bias rather than careful scholarship. The synoptic Gospels (Matthew, Mark, and Luke) along with the book of Acts were all written before 65 AD.[49] With such early

---

[48] William Lane Craig, *On Guard*, 233–234.
[49] This is even admitted by liberal scholar John A.T. Robinson who states that the overwhelming evidence reveals early dates for the synoptic Gospels and the book of Acts (by AD 60), giving only thirty years at the most between the time

and unanimous witness of the death, resurrection, and appearances of Christ, the logical explanation is that Jesus did actually rise from the dead bodily. To reject the historical evidence in favor of a late, poorly attested position simply because one feels he or she must hold to what he or she has been taught or was socially conditioned in is to act like the proverbial ostrich who sticks his head in the sand when confronted with the obvious. We dare not act like the Pharisees who stoned Stephen, plugging their ears and screaming at the top of their voices so they would not hear the truth (Acts 7:54–60). Jesus said, "The truth will set you free."[50] If the facts verify Christianity, then we will be held accountable for willfully rejecting those facts.

No other religion compares when you consider the miraculous nature of the Bible and the death and resurrection of Jesus. We can know what God is like by looking at Jesus (John 14:8–9). When all the evidence is weighed in, the sensible theist will embrace Christianity. And if this stuff is real, don't just go through the motions and half-heartedly worship God. Be an on-fire, radical disciple of Jesus. He is worth it, and you won't regret it.

---

of Christ and the writing of these works. John A.T. Robinson, *Can We Trust the New Testament?* (Grand Rapids: Eerdmans, 1977), 71–79. It is refreshing to see a scholar who doesn't believe in the miraculous advocate going with the evidence rather than coming up with an excuse in order to maintain his beliefs.

[50] John 8:31–32.

COMMON SENSE AND INTERPRETING THE BIBLE

Another important issue I want to discuss is how common sense can help us in interpreting the Bible. We have seen that it makes the most sense to believe that there is a God and that God is the God of the Bible. The Bible is trustworthy, but what if we interpret it incorrectly? Common sense tells us that what really matters is what God meant when He wrote His book. I hear a lot people say things like "What that passage means to me is…" As Americans, we think very highly of ourselves, but a little humility should be practiced. It doesn't matter what I think; what matters is what God thinks. Just like any book or letter, we should seek to discover what the original author meant to say, not what we want him or her to say. This is especially true with the Bible. What I am talking about now is called hermeneutics. Hermeneutics is the practice of proper interpretation skills to make sure we get from the Bible what God wants us to get. Common sense leads us to three basic principles of interpretation (hermeneutics) that help keep us honest and on the right path when it comes to understanding the Bible: (1) Discover what the original author intended to say to the original audience before you apply the passage to yourself. (2) As a literary work, the passage's genre must be considered. (3) Let the Bible interpret the Bible. Let's examine these three helps in a little more detail.

Original Intent

First, we must discover what the original author intended to say to the original audience before we apply the passage to our self. It is very possible to misinterpret the Bible if we don't get this first principle right. Think about it: the Bible was written between 1400 BC and AD 95 on three different continents, in three different languages (Hebrew, Greek, and Aramaic), by over forty different authors. Since we misinterpret each other, it is very likely we will misconstrue the authors of the Bible, unless we try to understand the individual prophet's culture and setting. Fortunately, because of archaeology, we have a good idea about the way the ancient biblical writers thought and lived. Good study tools can help us with culture and history so that we don't make mistakes.[51] For example, idioms are used by most every culture, but unless we understand the idiom, we can be confused. In America, we say "It's a piece of cake." Imagine an Asian just learning English hearing someone say "It's a piece of cake." He or she will say "What?" Let me give you an example of a Bible idiom. In Amos 4:6 (ESV), a literal translation says, "I gave you cleanness of teeth in all your cities." What should we think about this passage? God gave the Israelites good oral hygiene? Hardly! The CSB translates the same passage: "I gave you absolutely nothing to eat," and it includes a footnote that says, "Lit *you cleanness of teeth*." "Cleanness of teeth" is an idiom for being hungry, not dirtying your teeth with food.

Original intent answers a lot of the supposed problems people have trouble with. Article 13 in the Chicago Statement on Inerrancy states the following:

> We deny that it is proper to evaluate Scripture according to standards of truth and error that are alien to its usage or purpose. We further deny that inerrancy is negated by Biblical phenomena such as a lack of modern technical precision, irregularities of grammar or spelling, observational descriptions of nature, the reporting of falsehoods, the use of hyperbole and round numbers, the topical arrangement of metrical, variant

---

[51] I recommend the CSB Study Bible or the ESV Study Bible.

selections of material in parallel accounts, or the
use of free citations.[52]

This statement stems from the basic hermeneutical principle
that we are supposed to discover what the original author was trying
to say to the original audience in order to best understand what was
going on. If our level of precision was foreign to the original author,
then it would be inappropriate to force our precision on them. First-
century writers believed it was acceptable to rearrange events according to the theological point they were trying to make. Chronology
was not as important to them as it is to us. For instance, the order of
temptations is different due to what Matthew and Luke were trying
to say to their specific audiences. Matthew and Luke both cannot be
correct as far as chronology is concerned. We may ask, "So who was
correct?" Most scholars side with Matthew, but a case could also be
made for Luke being correct chronologically. The question to ask
would be, "Why would one or the other change the order?" Matthew's
account seems to present the temptations from least important to
most dramatic, ending with worship of Satan. If Matthew was seeking to make a dramatic presentation, he may have reordered Luke's
order to make that case; if that is the case, then Luke would be the
most accurate. But neither author was wrong in that they both presented the material in an acceptable first-century format. Similarly, in
a second example of a possible error, Matthew mentions good gifts,
while Luke mentions the Holy Spirit as the gift of the Father to those
who ask Him (Matthew 7:11; Luke 11:13). When we observe Luke
in general, it appears that the Holy Spirit is a major theme in his
writings. Mark mentions the Holy Spirit six times, Matthew twelve
times, Luke nineteen times, and Acts fifty-seven times (Luke wrote
Acts as well as Luke). In light of this observation, the original saying
was probably good gifts, and the Holy Spirit was added by Luke to
make his theological point, knowing that Jesus certainly meant this
as well. Free citations were acceptable to apostles as well. They didn't

---

[52] International Council on Biblical Inerrancy (ICBI), "The Chicago Statement
on Biblical Inerrancy" (1978), 8.

feel like they had to quote things in identical fashion as the actual speech, just so long as they presented the important truths accurately. The last example of a potential error I will give fits into this category. Was the divine voice speaking about Jesus (Matthew 3:17) or directly to Jesus (Luke 3:22)? It wasn't essential to the authors as to whether God was speaking about Jesus or directly to Jesus at the baptism; the important thing was what He said. In summary, we must be careful forcing our post-enlightenment demand of precision on a premodern people. What really matters is what the original authors meant to say to their original audiences. By the way, this is how we read all other literature.

Genre

Second, we need to recognize what type of literature is being used (in other words, what genre is the passage written in). The Bible has several genres and subgenres, so a few helps are necessary. Poetry uses exaggeration where poetic license is necessarily understood. Hosea 1:10 declares that "the number of Israelites will be like the sand of the sea, which cannot be measured or counted." We do not need to think that there will be trillions of Israelites; this is just a poetically expressive way of saying that there will be lots of them. In American songs, poetry is used, and most know not to take what is said literally. The same is true for Hebrew poetry. Personification is also used in poetry. Isaiah 55:12 says, "All the trees of the field will clap their hands." When we read this, we do not need to think that in heaven there will be trees clapping their branches as if they were Ents from *The Lord of the Rings*. Psalms uses a lot of poetry, but the prophets also utilize a lot of poetry. Other genres include law, wisdom, historical narrative, gospel, letters, and apocalyptic. God wrote the Bible in a variety of genres, revealing the beauty of the Bible but also lending to potential misinterpretation unless we recognize the genre.

Let the Bible Interpret the Bible

Finally, since God had the Bible written in a progressive fashion (He didn't tell us everything we need to know all at once), we should interpret difficult passages in light of clear passages and older, obscure verses in light of the fuller revelation made known later on. Since Jesus is the full revelation of God because He is God Himself and the plan of God, we interpret the Old Testament in light of the New Testament. For example, Jesus declared all foods clean according to Mark 7:19, so the Old Testament rules for food must be temporary. Hebrews 8:13 makes it clear: "By saying a new covenant, he has declared that the first is obsolete. And what is obsolete and growing old is about to pass away." Many of the laws of Moses were only temporary until Jesus came (Galatians 3:19–26); this is good news for those of us who like our pork ribs. But of course, we are still under the moral law of God found in both the Old and New Testament, because God doesn't change His moral standards.

You might ask, "Why did God write the Bible in this way?" I'm glad you asked. He wrote the book in such a way that it reaches transculturally across the world and throughout time but was written at a certain time through a specific culture. It's actually brilliant, which is what you would expect from deity. He chose a particular people (the family of Abraham) to bless the whole world (Genesis 12:3). We need to understand the specific culture and time so we don't misinterpret it but then see that it is transcultural and applicable to all people at all times, because God loves everyone!

Finally, in this last chapter, I want to deal with the most common objection to God and Christianity, the problem of evil and suffering. Obviously, there are more difficulties than just this one question, but this tends to be the one on most people's minds. For other questions, I recommend Paul Copan, who deals with a number of questions skeptics ask.

THE PROBLEM OF EVIL AND SUFFERING

The problem of evil is the most serious of all problems concerning God's existence. It has been expressed in many different ways. David Hume said, "Is he willing to prevent evil, but not able? Then he is impotent. Is he able, but not willing? Then he is malevolent. Is he both able and willing? Whence then is evil?"[53] Atheist Niclas Berggren states the theodicy problem as such:

1. If God exists, he is all-knowing, all-powerful, and perfectly good.
2. The existence of suffering is incompatible with the existence of God.
3. Suffering exists.
4. God does not exist.[54]

Though this is deductive reasoning (I will show how inductive reasoning is far better in the area of apologetics) and attacks theodicy (I will show that defense is superior to theodicy), it does show the

---

[53] As quoted in Alvin Plantinga, *God, Freedom, and Evil* (Grand Rapids: Eerdmans, 1974), p. 10.
[54] Niclas Berggren, *Does the Free-Will Defense Constitute a Sound Theodicy?* (Internet, Internet Infidels 1995–1997).

problem Christian apologists have to face. Ronald Nash puts it this way:

> Since evil and suffering exist, it seems to follow that it is reasonable to believe that God doesn't want to eliminate evil (thus casting doubt on his goodness) or doesn't know how to eliminate evil (raising questions about his knowledge) or lacks the power.[55]

Some people have rejected God's omnipotence because of this reasoning.[56] Others claiming to be evangelicals have rejected God's omniscience in the sense of his knowing the future in every detail. Richard Rice expresses this idea:

> As an aspect of his experience, God's knowledge of the world is also dynamic rather than static. Instead of perceiving the entire course of human existence in one timeless moment, God comes to know events as they take place. He learns something from what transpires. We call this position the "open view of God" because it regards God as receptive to new experiences and as flexible in the way he works toward his objectives in the world.[57]

These are serious deviations from orthodox Christianity as well as rational philosophy as even atheist Niclas Berggren pointed out in his first point. The problem of evil is serious, and an explanation is not easy. God is good, omnipotent (all-powerful), and omniscient

---

[55] Ronald Nash, *Faith and Reason* (Grand Rapids: Zondervan, 1988), p. 178.

[56] Harold Kushner, *When Bad Things Happen to Good People* (New York: Schocken Books, 1981).

[57] Clark Pinnock, etc., *The Openness of God* (Downers Grove: Inter Varsity Press, 1994), p. 16. The problem with this view is that it traps God in the box of time, but we have already seen that God created time.

(all-knowing). He does exist, and He does allow evil. We will see how all this can fit and how it is not irrational to believe in God even though evil is rampant in our world. First, we will look at different ways of dealing with the problem of evil, also noting the issues of deductive verses, inductive reasoning, and the difference between a theodicy and a defense. Next, we will look at the element of mystery. Third, we will look at the three defenses most commonly used for God's existence in the face of evil's existence. Finally, we will see how God has provided comfort and strength to live in a world filled with evil.

Different Ways of Dealing with the Problem of Evil

There are many different ways people deal with the problem of evil philosophically. The Zoroastrians, Manichaeists, and others have embraced dualism. This philosophy says that there are two eternal principles equal in strength locked together in conflict (like Star Wars). They say that good will eventually win, but this is in direct conflict with their basic philosophical presuppositions. If these two eternal principles have been battling for eternity, then they have had eternity to see if one can win, and therefore neither principle could ever win. This view is rejected by Christian philosophy because there is only one eternal Being who allowed evil to transpire. Think of it like this: what happens when an unstoppable force hits an immovable object? Obviously, one of them is not infinitely strong; this conundrum reveals that there can only be one infinite being. Dualism is found to be in error.

Another way of dealing with evil philosophically is to deny it. Hinduism as well as Christian science denies the actuality of evil, pain, and suffering. Hinduism teaches that all diversity and suffering are simply *maya* or illusion. This philosophy fails the pragmatic test. It doesn't work, and no one actually lives by it because pain and suffering are real. Christian philosophy rejects this philosophy as a form of escapism unfounded in Scripture or reason. In 1 Peter 4:19, it says, "So then, those who suffer according to God's will should commit themselves to their faithful Creator and continue to do good." It is clear that evil exists and, in some sense, God wills it.

The atheist's solution to the problem of evil is that there is no problem because there is no god. This not only does away with the problem; it also does away with evil. If there is no objective standard (God), then everything becomes relative. If everything is here by chance and will eventually be gone when the sun burns out, who's to say what I do to someone is morally significant? One could even argue that if we evolved by survival of the fittest, then for the strong to take advantage of the weak is only natural, not morally wrong. Intuition (a source of knowledge that is debatable but seems to be a self-evident truth) and conscience tells us that certain things are morally wrong. The Christian certainly must reject the atheist's solution because the Bible declares there is a God and there are morally binding laws on people (see Genesis 1:1). James Orr says the following:

> I lay it down as a first principle that, in the Christian view, sin is that which absolutely *ought not to be* (authors emphasis). How that which absolutely ought not to be is yet permitted to exist under the government of a wise and holy God, is a problem we may not be able to solve; but the first thing to do is to hold firmly to the conception of sin itself. Sin, as such, is that which unconditionally ought not to be, which contradicts or infringes upon an unconditional law of right, and therefore can only be understood in the light of that which ought to be—of the moral good.[58]

The Christian philosophy says there is a God and there is evil, but how do we show that there is no problem with the problem of evil? Before we look into the difficulty, we must state two preliminary

---

[58] James Orr, *The Christian View of God and the World* (Grand Rapids: Kregal, 1989 [originally published 1887]), p. 171.

ideas on how we will answer the problem. First, we must see that it is better as Christian apologists to argue inductively rather than deductively. Deductive arguments have the advantage of absolutely proving something, but they have the disadvantage that if the statement can't be shown to be absolutely true, it is thrown out. Inductive arguments show the reasonableness of an argument, but not the logical certainty; this is what I have been calling commonsense reasoning. There are some good arguments for the reasonableness of Christianity, and there are some difficulties (i.e., the problem of evil). The case for Christianity cannot be absolutely proven logically, but it can be shown to be highly probable. Blaise Pascal said, "There is enough light for those who only desire to see, and enough obscurity for those who have a contrary disposition."[59] There are some good answers to the problem of evil, but they are not logically certain answers. God has given enough evidence for the sincere seeker, but not enough to force the unwilling to capitulate. There is room for faith, though faith is founded on fact.[60] There is also a sense in which the problem of evil can be called an "inscrutable mystery."[61]

This leads us to the second preliminary idea that it is better to propose a defense rather than a theodicy. This idea was propounded by Alvin Plantinga, who says, "A theodicist, then, attempts to tell us why God permits evil. Quite distinct from a Free Will Theodicy *is* what I shall call a Free Will Defense. Here the aim is not to say what God's reason is, but at most what God's reason *might possibly be*."[62] A theodicy "seeks to 'justify the ways of God to man' (Milton), showing that God is in the right and is glorious and worthy of praise despite contrary appearances."[63] A defense merely seeks to show that

---

[59] As quoted in Bernard Ramm, *Varieties of Christian Apologetics* (Grand Rapids: Baker Books, 1962), p. 46.

[60] John Warwick Montgomery, *Faith Founded on Fact* (Newburg, Indiana: Trinity Press, 1978).

[61] Henri Blocher, *Evil and the Cross* (Downers Grove: Inter Varsity Press, 1994), p. 128.

[62] Alvin Plantinga, *God, Freedom, and Evil*, p. 28.

[63] Edited by Sinclair Ferguson, David Wright and J. I. Packer, *New Dictionary of Theology* (Downers Grove: Inter Varsity Press, 1988), p. 679.

the critic has not proven his or her case; it seeks to show that even under the difficulties, God's existence is possible. A defense burns the bridges that lead to disproving God's existence and leaves the building of new bridges that lead to accepting God's existence as probable to the positive apologetics (i.e., cosmological argument, teleological argument, moral argument, which I have previously covered). The theist only has to show the possibility of an explanation of why God allows evil, even though He is benevolent, all-powerful, and all-wise. He or she does not have to prove the explanation.

The Element of Mystery

A good defense for the Christian will consist of both biblical and philosophical persuasions. The Bible does not deal directly with the question, "How can a good, all-powerful God allow evil to run rampant in His universe?" The primary emphasis of Scripture is not the whys and origin of evil, but rather how to deal with evil and the end result of the eradication of evil. However, there are some implied understandings of Scripture that can be applied to our question. A major problem with the question itself is that it is anthropocentric rather than theocentric. If there is a God, then who are we to question His decisions? Job believed he was suffering unjustly. He did not understand the problem of suffering, which is a similar question to the problem of evil: how could a good, all-powerful God allow innocent people to suffer? Job demanded an interview with God so he could vindicate himself (Job 23:1–7). He gets the interview, but it doesn't go the way he expected. God does confront Job in Job 38–39. In rapid-fire succession, God questions Job to see if Job has enough knowledge to understand the question and even accuse God. In chapter 40:4–5, Job replies, "I am unworthy—how can I reply to you: I put my hand over my mouth. I spoke once, but I have no answer—twice, but I will say no more." God then barrages Job with more questions starting with the warning, "Brace yourself like a man; I will question you, and you shall answer me. Would you discredit my justice? Would you condemn me to justify yourself?" This is the question the proud atheist must answer as well. Job's final reply in 42:2–3 is worth noting:

> I know that you can do all things; no plan of yours can be thwarted. You asked, "Who is this that obscures my counsel without knowledge?" Surely I spoke of things I did not understand, things too wonderful for me to know.

Job admits that humans don't have enough data available and probably don't have the capacity to understand enough of all that the question entails to make a proper judgment. There is mystery involved in the question of why there is evil in this world because we probably don't have the capacity to understand (finiteness), and because we don't have the receptivity to understand (sinfulness). Deuteronomy 29:29 says, "The secret things belong to the LORD our God, but the things revealed belong to us and to our children forever, that we may follow all the words of this law." There are things God doesn't reveal to us. The Bible teaches that God is transcendent, meaning He is so far above and beyond us that unless He reveals Himself to us, we could not know anything about Him. The Bible also teaches that God is immanent, meaning that He has revealed Himself to us and is close to us. A part of His transcendence includes that His ways are not like our ways. Isaiah 55:8–9 says, "For my thoughts are not your thoughts, neither are your ways my ways, declares the LORD. As the heavens are higher than the earth, so are my ways higher than your ways and my thoughts than your thoughts." Isaiah 29:16 says, "You turn things upside down, as if the potter were thought to be like the clay! Shall what is formed say to him who formed it, 'He did not make me'? Can the pot say of the potter, 'He knows nothing'?" If there is a God, then to question His justice is blasphemy. If there is a God, then it makes sense that we would not be able to fully understand all His ways. That would only be possible if we were God, which we are not. If there is a God, then it is His standards of justice that are ultimate. This does not mean that God can change His standards or that He is above right and wrong. It does mean that right and wrong are not above Him. In fact, good is good because God is good; it is a part of His character. It is even impossible for God to lie because truthfulness is a part of His character (Hebrews 6:18). God's answer to a similar question as ours should cause a hesitancy to blurt out blasphemies: "But who are you, O man, to talk back to God? Shall what is formed say to him who formed it, 'why did you make me like this?'" Habakkuk asked a similar question to our question in Habakkuk 1:13: "Your eyes are too pure to look on evil; you cannot tolerate wrong. Why then do you tolerate the treacherous? Why are you silent while the wicked swallow up those more righteous than themselves?" God never gives him an answer, but He does speak to him. After speaking to Habakkuk, he responds in faith, recognizing God will bring about justice in the end and He will give him strength to endure in the meantime.[64] The problem of evil does not disprove God as we will see, and so we must practice humility and recognize our finiteness rather than rejecting God or judging God just because we don't understand Him. We are finite and sinful people, and therefore mystery must be allowed to enter the equation. Gerald Bray says, "Sin and the fall are realities which God has dealt with according to his wisdom. We may not understand their cause, but we have access to their cure, and it would obviously be silly to reject the latter simply because we cannot fully understand the former."[65] We will look at the cure later.

The philosophical defense of Christianity consists of three major defenses. These three defenses can be used to answer both deductive as well as inductive arguments against God. They do not prove the Christian position and therefore are not properly theodicies, but they do show that there are possible reasons for a good, all-powerful God to allow evil for a time.

---

[64] Habakkuk chapter 3.
[65] Gerald Bray, *The Doctrine of God* (Downers Grove: Inter Varsity Press, 1993), p. 92.

Answering the Deductive Problem of Evil

The atheologian claims that the biblical set of beliefs are contradictory at least implicitly because "If we add the at least initially plausible premises that good is opposed to evil in such a way that a being who is wholly good eliminates evil as far as he can, and that there are no limits to what an omnipotent being can do, then we do have a contradiction."[66] There are two parts to this accusation that are far from being proven in the deductive sense. First, are there no limits to what an omnipotent being can do? Rubel Shelly answers this question:

> Omnipotence is best understood as the ability to do anything that is not self-contradictory or in violation of moral perfection. To say that the deity is unable to make a rock so big he cannot lift it, an automobile whose dimensions are larger on the inside than the outside, a knife so sharp it can slice bread thinly enough to have only one side, or a round square is not to admit that things have been discovered that God *could* do if he had more power than he presently possesses... To say that God cannot act in violation of his own moral perfection is simply to insist that he cannot act contrary to his inherent qualities, which cause him to be good, and to wish all things to be like him insofar as possible.[67]

Second, is it true that a being who is wholly good will eliminate evil as far as he can? More than likely, Mackie means eliminate evil immediately because the Bible does teach that God will eventually eliminate evil. In fact, the Bible says God is waiting in order to

---

[66] J.L. Mackie as quoted in Ronald Nash, *Faith and Reason*, p. 182.
[67] Rubel Shelly, *Prepare To Answer* (Grand Rapids: Baker Book House, 1990), p. 78.

give more opportunity for people to accept His forgiveness so they won't be caught in judgment when God does eliminate evil.[68] Mackie probably means eliminate evil in the sense that it never exists. Ronald Nash gives a good summary of a Christian response to this problem:

> Suppose that it is logically possible for God to eliminate some evil, but the elimination of that evil would result either in the existence of a greater evil or in the nonexistence of a greater good. If I hit my thumb with a hammer, the resulting pain is an evil. Suppose a doctor tells me he can eliminate the throbbing in my thumb by amputating my hand at the wrist. While the doctor would have eliminated one evil, he would have done so at the cost of a much greater evil. There seem to be many evils in the world that can be eliminated only by producing situations containing more evil or costing us some greater good. Suppose that many evils result from human free will or from the fact that our universe operates under natural laws or from the fact that humans exist in a setting that fosters soul-making. And suppose further that a world containing free will and natural law that fosters soul-making contains more good than a world that does not. If it makes no sense for God to eliminate an evil that would bring about a state of affairs in which there would be less good or more evil, our newest candidate for the missing proposition—that a good being always eliminates evil as far as it can—may safely be dismissed as neither true nor an essential Christian belief.[69]

---

[68] 2 Peter 3:8–9.
[69] Ronald Nash, *Faith and Reason*, p. 186.

In an inductive defense of Christianity rather than a deductive theodicy, the Christian only has to show a possible solution to the problem. It certainly cannot be proven that a supreme being could not have a good reason to allow evil for a time, namely that eliminating the evil prematurely would bring about a greater evil or eliminate a greater good in the process of eliminating the evil.

The inductive problem of evil is formidable. This is a move from the claim that theism is illogical and proven to be false because of the existence of evil to the claim that theism is probably false due to the quantity of evil in the world. We will now deal with the inductive problem of evil with three defenses (which also work for the deductive problem of evil).

Free Will Defense

The first and best defense is the free will defense, which we will call FWD. As a theodicy, free will has been used for centuries, but with legitimate rebuttals. Free will does not prove God's existence in spite of the presence of evil, but as a defense, it does give a possible reason why God allows evil. Dan Story states the FWD well:

> God created Adam (and all people) to worship, obey, and have fellowship with Him—to love Him. Genuine love is inseparable from free will. God could have created Adam, and all other people, to think and act like robots. By divine mandate, God could have caused Adam not only to obey Him but to love Him. Would this have been genuine love? Of course not. Love can't be programmed; it must be freely expressed. God wanted Adam to show his love by freely choosing obedience. That's why God gave Adam a free will. A free choice, however, leaves the possibility

of a wrong choice. Adam made the wrong choice,
thereby allowing sin to enter the world.[70]

God allowed evil into this world possibly because it was the
only way possible for the greater good of having people that freely
choose to love Him and each other. Hugh Ross says, "Without the
element of free choice there wouldn't be the possibility for the expression of love—we would literally be robots."[71] He gives the illustration
of how a person could program their computer to tell the person
it loves them, even with loving intonations, but it is just not the
same as that person's wife telling him she loves him. Love demands
freedom and freedom demands the possibility of evil. Berggren gives
three arguments against the FWD:

1. FWD does not cover nonmoral evils.
2. People don't have free will according to the Bible.
3. God could have made people free without choosing evil.[72]

We will answer these objections in reverse order. The third argument is well stated in the form of a question by J. L. Mackie: "If God
has made men such that in their free choices they sometimes prefer
what is good and sometimes what is evil, why could he not have
made men such that they always freely choose the good?"[73] Mackie
seems to misunderstand what it means to freely choose. Plantinga
explains, "Now God can create free creatures, but He can't *cause* or
determine them to do only what is right. For if He does so, then they
aren't significantly free after all; they do not do what is right *freely*."[74]
Plantinga goes on to say that it is possible that "God is omnipotent,
and it was not within His power to create a world containing moral

---

[70] Dan Story, *Defending Your Faith* (Nashville: Thomas Nelson, 1992), p.
170–172.
[71] Hugh Ross, Video "How Could A Loving God…?" (Pasadena: Reasons to
Believe, 1992).
[72] Niclas Berggren, Internet article.
[73] As quoted in Ronald Nash, *Faith and Reason*, p. 190.
[74] Alvin Plantinga, *God, Freedom, and Evil*, p. 30.

good but no moral evil."[75] We have already seen that God's omnipotence does not mean He can do absolutely anything including the logically impossible. Creating free humans that will choose to do good always is logically impossible because He would have to make them choose the good, which takes away from their freedom.

Berggren's second argument is that people don't have free will if they are born with a sinful nature. This is certainly a problem for the pure Calvinist. R. K. Wright, is a Calvinist who rejects the FWD. He says the following:

> God is the first cause of everything that happens (including all evils), because as the Creator he causes "whatsoever comes to pass." "Second causes" are the later things in the sequence of events (like Satan, Adam or me), from whom sins directly proceed. These secondary causes are the author(s) of sin because they are the direct causes of it. According to the Westminster Confession, God is holy and separated from my sin by not being the direct cause (or author) of it. A cause may be ultimate (of which God is the original cause) or it may be proximate, such as the sinner. Therefore the sinner, not God, is the author of sin for the same reason that a father is not the author of his son's book.[76]

First of all, Wright's example of a father not being the author of his son's book is a non sequitur. His father was not the first cause of the book. But this argument is also silly and makes God the author of sin. If in billiards I shoot the white ball and it hits the eight ball into the corner pocket, it is certainly not the white ball's fault as the secondary cause. It is my fault as the first cause. If I hire a hit man

---

[75] Ibid., p. 45.
[76] R.K. McGregor Wright, *No Place for Sovereignty* (Downers Grove: Inter Varsity Press, 1996), p. 200.

to kill someone, I am at fault, even though I was not the immediate cause of the death. If God causes us to do evil, then He is the author of evil and is guilty. But James 1:13 says, "When tempted, no one should say, 'God is tempting me.' For God cannot be tempted by evil, nor does he tempt anyone." Matthew 18:6 says, "But if anyone causes one of these little ones who believe in me to sin, it would be better for him to have a large millstone hung around his neck and to be drowned in the depths of the sea." This would certainly be true of God as well as humans. If the doctrine of original sin strips humans of free will in all senses of the term, then it does hinder the FWD. But humans don't always choose to sin. Total depravity (the result of the sinful nature we inherit from Adam) does not mean we are as bad as we could be. We do, in some sense, still have a limited free will. If the idea of prevenient grace is true, then it is possible for God to bring us to a place of freedom of choice (like Adam) even after we sin when the Word of God comes in the power of the Spirit. This idea is accepted by Arminians and even some Calvinists (i.e., Millard Erickson[77]). Also, it is not at all clear that the enlightenment view of the autonomy of humans, including radical individualism, is true. We are our brother's keeper, and we are all in this together as even social Darwinists would concede. James Orr states the following:

> The former idea, at all events, is now thoroughly incorporated into modern habits of thinking, under the name of the "solidarity" of the race. There is an individual life, and there is a social life in which we all share. The race is an organism, and the individual, if we may so speak, is a cell in the tissue of that organism, indissolubly connected for good or evil with the other cells in the unity of a common life. From this follows the conception of heredity, which plays so important a part in modern theories. Man is not simply

---

[77] Millard Erickson, *Christian Theology* (Grand Rapids: Baker Book, 1985), pp. 930–933 though Erickson would call it effectual calling and see it as irresistible.

bound up with his fellows through the external usages and institutions of society. He has been produced by, and has become a part of them... he is organically related to all the members of the race, not only bone of their bone and flesh of their flesh, but mind of their mind. He is a bundle of inherited tendencies, and will in turn transmit his nature, with its new marks of good and evil, to those who come after him. It is easy to see that this conception of heredity, and of the organic unity of the race, is but the scientific expression of a doctrine which is fundamental to the Scriptures, and which underlies all its teaching about sin and salvation.[78]

Would it have been better for God to have created autonomous, individualistic, non-interdependent humans? I doubt it. We are in this together. The Bible does say I will not be eternally punished for someone else's sin (including Adam's) in Ezekiel chapter 18. Prevenient grace seems to be a biblical option (Acts 16:14).[79] Therefore, the doctrine of original sin does not hinder the FWD.

The last problem Berggren had with the FWD is that it does not cover nonmoral evils such as earthquakes, hurricanes, etc. It is certainly true that the world is messed up. The "creation was subjected to frustration" and longs to be "liberated from its bondage to decay" (Romans 8:20–21). A curse has been placed on this earth because of Adam's sin (Genesis 3:17–18). What we call natural evils can be direct punishment by God on humanity (the flood in Genesis 6) or indirect tragedy on humanity because of the curse's pervasive nature or even blessings in disguise. Also, much of what Berggren calls nonmoral evil is actually moral evil caused by Satan and his demons. This is what Gregory Boyd calls a "warfare worldview":

---

[78] James Orr, *The Christian View of God and the World*, p. 169-170.
[79] See Thomas Oden, *The Transforming Power of Grace* (Nashville: Abingdon Press, 1993), chapter two.

Stated most broadly, this worldview is that perspective on reality which centers on the conviction that the good and evil, fortunate or unfortunate, aspects of life are to be interpreted largely as the result of good and evil, friendly or hostile, spirits warring against each other and against us.[80]

Though this answer might seem repugnant to enlightened people, it is certainly not illogical. Einstein postulated the possibility of up to eleven dimensions of space and time. Who's to say there isn't an unseen realm where angels and demons reside? How else can we account for the amount of evil in humanity? Hugh Ross says the following:

Many who argue that the existence of evil and suffering proves the nonexistence of an all-powerful, all-loving Creator have no idea that it proves just the opposite. Naturalistic materialism, the notion that the natural world accounts for itself and needs no outside explanation, cannot account for the evil and cruelty we see among humans. Survival of the fittest does not result in the behavior humans exhibit all over the planet toward the land itself and toward animals and fellow humans.[81]

When we look at Satanism; voodoo; mass murderers; and world leaders like Hitler, Pol Pot, and Idi Amin, it is not too far-fetched to say they might be possessed. Ravi Zacharias gives an illustration of someone converting to Christianity after seeing the amount of evil in this world:

---

[80] Gregory Boyd, *God at War* (Downers Grove: Inter Varsity Press, 1997), p. 13.
[81] Hugh Ross, *Beyond the Cosmos* (Colorado Springs: NavPress, 1996), p. 176.

One of the most remarkable conversions to Christianity was that of the poet W.H. Auden... Jacobs narrates an event in 1940 when Auden entered a predominantly German section of a movie theater in Manhattan where the Third Reich's filmed version of its conquest of Poland was being shown. To the sheer shock and dismay of Auden, every time a Pole would appear on the scene, the angry screams of the crowd would resound in the theater. "Kill him...Kill them!" they would shout, somewhat reminiscent of the bloodthirsty cries of the Roman masses as they thronged the arena to witness the gladiatorial orgies of savagery and sadism.

Auden left the theater tremendously shaken and confounded by this experience of unmitigated hatred he had witnessed. His dismay lay not merely in his inability within his humanistic framework to find a solution to such a moral plague, but in his obvious inability to even explain the existence of such inhuman passions holding the mind in its grasp. He was having difficulty "spelling" evil, given his presuppositions. That struggle led to his Christian conversion, which coherently provided an explanation both to the depravity of man and an answer for its cure.[82]

The plausible idea of Satan and his demons who rebelled against God before humanity's rebellion answers both the problem of non-moral evil as well as the extent of evil. One last thing in response to the extent of evil being a problem is shown below:

---

[82] Ravi Zacharias, *Can Man Live Without God?* (Dallas, Word, 1994), pp. 48–49.

Before we begin to worry that there might be too much evil in the world, we need to answer a number of preliminary questions: Is there a limit to the amount of evil we might reasonably expect to find in a world created by God? What precisely is that limit? How might anyone arrive at a knowledge of that limit? Of course, there are no answers to these questions. And since there aren't, there is no objective means by which anyone could determine that a reasonable quantity of evil in the world had been exceeded. Claims that the existence of God is somehow made less plausible because of the quantity of evil in the world rest on the quicksand of subjective opinion.[83]

Finally, what Berggren calls moral evil might be good. Earthquakes, hurricanes, wildfires, volcanic eruptions, comet and asteroid collisions, disease, cancer, and pandemics are all optimized to maximally benefit terrestrial life in the context of the laws of physics. The laws of physics and the cosmic space-time dimensions are part of God's tools to ensure that the maximum possible number of free will humans choose eternal life with Him rather than eternal life without Him. The laws of physics and the space-time dimensions are designed by God as tools in his hands to bring about a rapid, efficient eradication of evil and suffering while enhancing the capacity of humans who choose His redemptive offer to experience and express love (the greater good). Note that the present laws of physics are temporary. They remain in place only until the full number of humans God intends to redeem have in fact been redeemed. In the new creation, there will be no thermodynamics, electromagnetism, and gravity (Romans 8, Revelation 21).[84]

---

[83] Ronald Nash, *Faith and Reason*, p. 198.
[84] See Hugh Ross, *Why the Universe is the Way it is* (Baker Books: Grand Rapids, 2008) for more on this.

The FWD can really be seen as a part of the Greater Good Defense or GGD. Doug Erlandson defines the GGD: "A being is not morally culpable in allowing preventable evil if he has a 'morally sufficient reason' for so doing."[85] Once again in a defense, as opposed to a theodicy, one only has to show the plausibility of the argument, not the actuality of it. I include the FWD in with the GGD because the greater good that comes out of free will is love. If love is forced, it is really rape, not love. When we are allowed freedom to love, we also have the option not to love. God deemed this love relationship with us important enough to allow the possibility of evil. This love relationship is seen as ultimate in importance to God when we see what He deems as the greatest commandment of all and thus the most important commandment of all. A Pharisee asked Jesus, "Teacher, which is the greatest commandment in the Law?" and Jesus responded, "Love the Lord your God with all your heart and with all your soul and with all your mind. This is the first and greatest commandment."[86]

To freely love God is a greater good that gives reason for why God would allow evil, even the amount we see in the world, for a time. This GGD also gives reasons for why there is not absolute proof for God's existence. If there was so much evidence that it would demand the unwilling to capitulate, there would be no reason for a loving response. This may be why God doesn't perform more miracles than what we see. God gives plenty of evidence for the sincere seeker to find Him, but not so much that the disinclined would be forced to believe.

The proposition above has been shown to be possible, and therefore the atheologian has been answered. Even if the FWD is rejected, the problem of evil can still be answered from a defense perspective. We don't have to know what God's reason is for allowing evil. We just need to know that it is not illogical that God could have a reason for allowing evil. Paul Helm, who rejects the FWD, says,

---

[85] Doug Erlandson, "A New Perspective on the Problem of Evil" (Internet: www.wavefront.com/~contra_m/antithesis/v2n2/ant_v2n2_evil.html), p. 1.

[86] Matthew 22:36–37.

"One is that God has a good reason for permitting or ordaining evil, but that none of us has an inkling what that good reason is."[87] We have much more than an inkling. Two other defenses can be added to the arsenal of the theist. They do not prove God's existence on their own, but they do compliment the FWD: The Natural Law Defense (NLD) and the Soul-Making Defense (SMD).

Natural Law Defense

The NLD is defined by Ronald Nash (he actually defines the Natural Law Theodicy, but for our purposes we will use the same definition): "The natural law theodicy states that the existence of a lawlike and orderly creation is a necessary condition for a number of divine objectives. Just as it makes sense to believe that God endowed humans with significant moral freedom, it is also reasonable to believe that God placed these free moral agents in a universe exhibiting order."[88] In an orderly universe, if the natural laws are broken, consequences must follow. If someone shoots me with a bullet, it will rip into my body and hurt me. Some might complain and say, "Why didn't God create a different universe?" But no one has been able to show the possibility of this alternative universe. Others may say, "Why doesn't God intervene when bad is about to happen?" God indeed does intervene at times, but if He intervened at all times, there would be no order, only a destabilized world where free and responsible actions would be impossible. If God intervened at all times, it would blunt the crucial role of thermodynamics, gravity, and electromagnetism in motivating us to avoid evil and pursue virtue. In chapter 10 of *Why the Universe Is the Way It Is,* Ross describes eleven distinct purposes for God creating the universe. God knows what He is doing.

---

[87] Paul Helm, *The Providence of God* (Downers Grove: Inter Varsity Press, 1994), p. 200.
[88] Ronald Nash, *Faith and Reason,* p. 200.

Soul-Making Defense

The final compliment to the FWD is the SMD. Nash defines the SMD: "The soul-making theodicy states that in order for God to produce the virtuous beings with whom he wants fellowship, these individuals must face challenges that teach them the intrinsic worth of the virtues he possesses perfectly."[89] John Frame counters this, stating the statement below:

> However, I think that it is unbiblical to turn this principle into a full-scale theodicy. For one thing, Scripture teaches that Adam was not created morally immature with a need to develop character through suffering. He was created good, and had he obeyed God, he would not have needed to experience suffering.[90]

The SMD cannot be used as a theodicy or even as a defense unless it is accompanied by the FWD. But with the FWD, it makes sense. Most would agree that the spoiled brat who is spared all pain and difficulty lacks good character. Character, like muscles is developed with difficulty—"No pain, no gain." Suffering develops character. The SMD and the NLD fit the FWD well. In many cases, suffering can result in good. It helps build patience and character. The student who suffers through poverty to finish his education will benefit in the end. The disease of leprosy shows the necessity of pain. Pain is a warning system in our body to alert us of danger. Because the leper has no pain system, he destroys his body unknowingly. Philip Yancey gives an excellent example of what can happen when we resist the blessing of pain:

---

[89] Ibid., p. 204.
[90] John Frame, *Apologetics to the Glory of God* (Phillipsburg, New Jersey: P and R Publishing, 1994), p. 164.

A tragic example of someone not heeding the warning occurred in an NBA basketball game in which a star player, Bob Gross, wanted to play despite a badly injured ankle. Knowing that Gross was needed for the important game, the team doctor injected Marcaine, a strong pain-killer, into three different places of his foot. Gross did start the game, but after a few minutes, as he was battling for a rebound, a loud *snap!* could be heard throughout the arena. Gross, oblivious, ran up and down the court two times, then crumpled to the floor. Although he felt no pain, a bone had broken in his ankle. By overriding pain's warning system with the anesthetic, the doctor caused permanent damage to Gross's foot and ended his basketball career. Pain is not God's great goof. The sensation of pain is a gift—the gift that nobody wants.[91]

In my role as a professor, universities pay me to make my students suffer. Amazingly, my students are eager to pay money to suffer at my hand. Why? They understand the greater good that will come from this suffering. Furthermore, they understand that there will be no gratuitous suffering. They also understand that there is no other way to gain this greater good. God knew what He was doing when He created pain.

Two Further Problems Answered

Albert Camus asked the question that if suffering is God's will, then when we try to stop suffering (i.e., hospitals, medicine, etc.), we are fighting God. This can be answered when we realize God permits evil rather than causes it. God has both a permissive will and a causative

---

[91] Philip Yancey, *Where Is God When It Hurts?* (Grand Rapids: Zondervan, 1990), p. 34.

will. Sometimes, God causes what we might consider evil as punishment. When He does, it cannot logically be called evil because it is justice, and justice is good. Sometimes, God allows evil in the world to bring about the greater good (GGD, FWD). In this sense, He doesn't cause it. When we understand this, Francis Schaeffer's response to Camus is justified:

> We can fight evil without fighting God, because
> God did not make things as they are now—as
> man in his cruelty has made them. God did not
> make man cruel, and He did not make the results
> of man's cruelty. These are abnormal, contrary
> to what God made, and so we can fight the evil
> without fighting God.[92]

Another question some have is that if in heaven we don't have evil, why didn't God create us in heaven in the first place? And if we have free will in heaven, then who's to say we won't choose evil again? When we freely choose God's way of salvation, we also freely give up our freedom. Romans 6:20–22 says the following:

> When you were slaves to sin, you were free from
> the control of righteousness. What benefit did
> you reap at that time from the things you are
> now ashamed of? Those things result in death!
> But now that you have been set free from sin and
> have become slaves to God, the benefit you reap
> leads to holiness, and the result is eternal life.

We must recognize that our past freedom to sin was actually a slavery to sin. But when we are saved, we voluntarily become slaves to righteousness, no longer free to sin. When we make Jesus our Lord, we give up our freedom, but it is worth it. It is like marriage. Before

---

[92] Francis Schaeffer, *The Complete Works of Francis Schaeffer* (Westchester: Crossway Books, 1982), Vol. 1, p. 301.

we get married, we decide to love and cherish our future spouse. When we get married, we can no longer decide to love someone else the same way we commit to love our spouse. We give up our freedom, but it is worth it. But we need the freedom before the marriage; otherwise, it is not love. Our relationship to God is actually likened to a marriage in Revelation 19.

But the argument still goes that If God is all-powerful, then why doesn't He get rid of evil? Let's suppose that you are God, and you have the ability to make the decree to annihilate all evil. What would happen when you made that decree? For one thing, you would be gone because you still have evil selfishness within you. Everyone else would also be annihilated because we are all selfish, and we all sin against what we know to be right. So do you see the difficulty with our easy solutions? Walter Martin makes an excellent point in discussing this problem:

> If God interferes in our world and stops everything right now, man becomes autonotoms because only a sovereign decree superseding all human rights of choice can halt the evil which is within our nature exercising itself. But if he chooses not to do that and permits us to go on with evil then we raise our voices and our fists to heaven and we say, "You're cruel and inhuman and unjust, because you have the power to do it and you won't." Either way God can never win. If he interferes, we are robots and we are no longer free, and we protest. And if he doesn't interfere, he is guilty because he doesn't use his omnipotence to stop us. Our solutions never work. That's why we must look at it from the perspective of heaven.[93]

---

[93] Martin, Walter. The Existence of God. San Juan Capistrano, California: Christian Research Institute, 1980 (Cassette).

Pastoral Considerations

The above arguments entail the philosophical problem of evil. This is not very comforting to the person who is existentially experiencing evil. As I said before, the Bible does not deal so much with the whys of evil as it does with the solutions to evil. I would like to conclude with four helps for those in the midst of the struggle.

First, don't blame God. This is our first inclination, but it only compounds the problem. We have the freedom to choose our course in life. We do not have absolute freedom due to our situation in life, but we do have a limited but real freedom. In order to be free, the possibility of choosing against God's will must be allowed; this results in evil. God allowed the possibility of evil, but we brought it about by our choice. It is wrong to blame God for evil; we must blame ourselves.

> Imagine this scenario: vandals break into a museum displaying works from Picasso's Blue Period. Motivated by sheer destructiveness, they splash red paint all over the paintings and slash them with knives. It would be the height of unfairness to display these works—a mere sampling of Picasso's creative genius, and spoiled at that—as a representative of the artist. The same applies to God's creation. God has already hung a "Condemned" sign above the earth, and has promised judgment and restoration. That this world spoiled by evil and suffering still exists at all is an example of God's mercy, not his cruelty.[94]

Freedom of choice is necessary for real love to be possible.

> In a perfectly fair world, morality would operate according to fixed laws, just like the laws of

---

[94] Philip Yancey, *Where Is God When It Hurts?* p. 67–68.

nature. Punishment for wrongdoing would work like physical pain. If you touch a flame, you are "punished" instantly with a pain warning; a fair world would punish sin just that swiftly and surely. Extend your hand to shoplift, and you'd get an electrical shock. Likewise, a fair world would reward good behavior: Fill out an IRS form honestly, and you'd earn a pleasure sensation, like a trained seal given a fish.

That imaginary world has a certain appeal. It would be just and consistent, and everyone would clearly know what God expected. Fairness would reign. There is, however, one huge problem with such a tidy world: it's not at all what God wants to accomplish on earth. He wants from us love, freely given love, and we dare not underestimate the premium God places on that love. Freely given love is so important to God that he allows our planet to be a cancer of evil in his universe—for a time.[95]

The second thing we need to understand is that God is waiting for a good reason. In 2 Peter 3:9, it says, "The Lord is not slow in keeping his promise, as some understand slowness. He is patient with you, not wanting anyone to perish, but everyone to come to repentance." If Jesus would have come back before January of 1976, I would not have the eternal life God promises to those who believe. I don't mind the suffering I endure now because I know that others will receive this wonderful gift of eternal life.

The third thing we need to understand is that Jesus is coming back someday, and therefore suffering and evil are only temporary. Though seventy years of pain, even sheer torture, is difficult, it is bearable when seen in the light of eternity. Seventy years is a blip on the timeline of eternity, next to nonexistent. After a few billion years

---

[95] Ibid., p. 90.

in eternal bliss with God, our pain will be a distant memory. Our hope is in the coming of Jesus, not in this life (though as we will see, God comforts us in this life). Right now, God is allowing evil to run its course so we can see that God's will is the best choice and so that as many as possible can be saved from evil's clutches. The origin of evil may be mysterious, but its outcome is certain: justice and love shall overcome and reign for eternity. Christianity offers resources for coping with pain and overcoming evil, so even though evil exists, we have not been abandoned, and we are given a hope of deliverance from it.

> Joni Eareckson Tada tells of a time when she visited a home for the mentally retarded. Usually when she visits a care facility and recounts her life story, speaking from a wheelchair, she keeps her audience spellbound. These patients, however, of varying ages but all with undeveloped minds, had trouble with attention span. When Joni reached the part about imagining what heaven would be like, she could tell she had lost their interest entirely.
>
> It was a warm day, and Joni could feel perspiration rolling down her body as she struggled to continue. Finally, in desperation, she said this, "And heaven will be the place where all of you will get new minds." As soon as the words came out, she regretted them—what if they sounded paternalistic, or cruel? But instantly the atmosphere in the room changed. Spontaneously, the patients started cheering, with loud applause. Joni had tapped into their deepest hope.[96]

Christians are not promised a life without suffering, but suffering is seen as temporary. We may suffer horrendously for seventy

---

[96] Ibid., p. 214.

years or so, but we are promised an eternity without suffering. When seen in this light, suffering can be endured. Any philosophy must deal with death. Sigmund Freud wrote, "And finally there is the painful riddle of death, for which no remedy at all has yet been found, nor probably ever will be."[97] Aristotle said, "Death is a dreadful thing, for it is the end."[98] Apart from the hope given in Christianity, the future is very bleak for humankind. Of course, if Christianity is not true, then what I have said is also not true. All I have shown is the pragmatic value of Christianity. But the hope given in Christianity does help us understand and cope with the riddle of pain, suffering, and evil.

The final thing I would say about evil and suffering is that we can receive the comfort and strength of the Holy Spirit right now to help us cope until Jesus returns. John 14:16–18, 27 says below:

> And I will ask the Father, and he will give you another Counselor [comforter, advocate] to be with you forever—the Spirit of truth. The world cannot accept him, because it neither sees him nor knows him. But you know him, for he lives with you and will be in you. I will not leave you as orphans; I will come to you... Peace I leave with you; my peace I give you. I do not give to you as the world gives. Do not let your hearts be troubled and do not be afraid.

God will give us the comfort and strength we need to endure until He wipes out all evil and suffering (John 14:1–4).

---

[97] As quoted in Warren Wiersbe, *Be Wise: 1 Corinthians* (Wheaton, Illinois: Victor Books, 1988), p. 155.

[98] As quoted in James Stewart, *A Faith to Proclaim* (London.: Hadder and Stoughton, 1953), p. 135.

CONCLUSION

Common sense tells us that there is a God who has written a book to show us how to live and how to be saved. That book is the Bible. God has a plan for us, but our sin keeps us from that plan. God's plan has not been thwarted because God sent His Son to this earth to die on the cross so that our sins could be forgiven and we could be reconciled to Him. He always wanted a relationship with us. Common sense tells us that God is so powerful that He obviously doesn't need servants. He wants people who will choose to receive His love and love Him as their God. Common sense also tells us that God is both holy and loving. He will judge those who refuse His offer of forgiveness and reconciliation. If there is a God, and there is, and if He has written a book explaining to us who He is and what His plan is, and He has, then it makes sense that we will drop everything and read that book and follow that God. Whenever Jesus called anyone, He said "Follow me." If you have been convinced by what I have said, then I would suggest you start out with a prayer and then follow Him. You could say something like this: "God, I am a sinner. I don't deserve your forgiveness, but I ask you to forgive me. I believe Jesus died on the cross for my sins. I am trusting in Jesus now, not myself or my good works. I surrender to you as Lord. Whenever I have been in charge of my life, I have blown it. I know that sin has wrecked this world, including my sins. I repent of my sins, and I place my faith in Jesus and what He has done for me on the cross. Thank you for the gift of eternal life. Amen." To follow Him, you start out by getting baptized. Next, continue to read the Bible every day along with prayer. Find a good Bible-believing church and get actively involved in it. Share with others the decision you have made to follow Jesus.

He is coming back someday, so be prepared ahead of time. That is common sense!

Perhaps you have not been convinced beyond a reasonable doubt. You would say to me, "Larry, you haven't proven to me this stuff is real. If I am going to surrender my whole life, I need more evidence." I don't blame you. I have been attempting to remove any unnecessary intellectual boulders  that might get in the way of your faith, but you still need to take the step of faith necessary for salvation. For more evidence, I would encourage you to look up the resources I have mentioned in the footnotes. I would also encourage you to ask God to reveal Himself to you. Go to church with an open mind and heart; seek God in solitude. Read the Bible, starting with the Gospel of John. I believe God will reveal Himself to you. He met with me some thirty-five years ago, and my life has never been the same. He is just as real to me as the people I see walking around our planet. Since I have started my journey with God, I have seen several people miraculously healed. I have seen totally messed up people set free from their bondages. I have seen broken marriages restored. I have seen hopeless people filled with the joy and peace that comes from knowing God. He is real. He has spoken. Are you listening?

Blaise Pascal is attributed to what is called the wager argument. It basically goes like this: There is a lot of evidence for the existence of God and the reality of Christianity. There are some questions people propose, like "How can an all-loving, all-powerful God allow evil and suffering in the world?" There are good answers to the tough questions, so the negative doesn't negate the positive. Everyone makes a choice, by either surrendering to God through Christ or not. There is no neutral ground. If you are not following Jesus, you are not following Jesus. Sounds redundant, but we have to be obvious to some people who are actually practical atheists. They say they believe, but they live as if there is no God. Since we haven't proven one hundred percent that there is a God, everyone makes a wager. You bet with your life that He either exists or doesn't. If you bet He exists and He ends up not existing, you really haven't lost much. Christians tend to be happier than non-Christians. You end up ceasing to exist, which is what happens to atheists too if they are right. But if you bet He doesn't exist and He actually does exist, then you really pay a stiff penalty—hell forever. Common sense says, "Keep seeking God, because the potential consequences are huge!"

ABOUT THE AUTHOR

Dr. Larry Siekawitch is senior pastor at Harvest Fellowship in Sauk Rapids, Minnesota. He is also professor of Bible and theology at the University of Northwestern–Saint Paul. Larry has pastored for over twenty-five years and taught at the college level for over thirteen years. He has taught classes in apologetics, worldviews, ethics, systematic, biblical and historical theology, as well as multiple Bible courses. His PhD is in historical theology, and his passion is to share Christ with those who have difficulties believing. His spiritual gifts are teaching, evangelism, and leadership. He has been in two professional debates: one with a Muslim scholar at Saint Cloud State University on the Bible compared to the Qur'an, and the other with the famous atheist Dan Barker in Colorado Springs on the existence of God. He is happily married to his wife, Elizabeth, for over thirty years and has three grown sons, Daniel, Isaac, and Mark. He has previously written *The Uniqueness of the Bible* and *Balancing Head and Heart in Seventeenth Century Puritanism*. Larry is a member of both the Evangelical Theological Society and Reasons to Believe Scholar Community. One of his favorite verses is 1 Peter 3:15, which says, "But in your hearts regard Christ the Lord as holy, ready at any time to give a defense to anyone who asks you for a reason for the hope that is in you. Yet do this with gentleness and respect." People deserve answers to their questions and to be treated with respect; this book does both.

CPSIA information can be obtained
at www.ICGtesting.com
Printed in the USA
LVHW030433021220
673097LV00007B/347